094   LEE

Pearson's Railway

LEEDS · SETTLE · CARLISLE

HERTFORDSHIRE
LIBRARY SERVICE

No
H31 127 365 9

Class
385.09427

Supplier	Price	Date
FARRIES	5.95	7-10-91

ublished b................................Common,
taffordshi........................13674.

Michael ....ll rights Res

rst edition 1991. 0 907864 57 0

Cartogra...y by Malcolm Barnes of Burton-upon-Trent.

.....tion by ....ical Graphics of ...nton.

.... The Matthews Wright Pres.. Chard, Somerset.

D1465243

SEP 1995

33

SALTAIRE. *"imitation gas lamps, Midland look-alike diagonal fencing, flower baskets and trim stone waiting shelters . . ."*

LEEDS, SETTLE & CARLISLE –
The Story So Far

NOT JUST A RAILWAY, more a national monument, the Settle & Carlisle survived as many assassination attempts as the head of a Third World junta to become a profit-making tourist attraction 'visited' by half a million people a year. Mean, moody and magnificent, it is the Jane Russell of railways, thrusting its way through the burgeoning fells of the Yorkshire Dales, across a landscape not unreminiscent of the film star's own memorable contours. It has been mentioned in the same haunted company as Hadrian's Wall and York Minster and it has been labelled one of the great railway journeys in the world. And yet if it is a monument to Victorian optimism and imagination, the Settle & Carlisle is also a monument to misplaced pride, to the parsimony of accountancy-led decision-making, and to the folly of country which has never had an integrated transport policy.

THE story of the Settle & Carlisle has more ironies than a Shakespearian drama. Its origins date back to the middle of the 19th century and the ambitious Midland Railway's attempts to tap the market for trade and traffic between London, the Midlands and Scotland. The company's rivalry with the London & North Western Railway and the latter's brinkmanship with regard to advertised connections at the Dales village of Ingleton are part of railway history. Passengers booked through to Scotland were often made to walk between the Midland's station at Ingleton and the London & North Western's in order to catch a connecting train. What through carriages there were, were attached to the slowest of LNWR trains. Frustrated by such delaying tactics, the Midland directors announced an intention to build their own independent route to Carlisle, where they would link up with the Glasgow & South-Western to Glasgow and the North British to Edinburgh. Scarcely believing that the Midland would be mad enough to build a line across the Pennine wilderness, the London & North Western called their bluff. In response, and so as not to lose face, the Midland passed an Act of Parliament for the construction of a seventy-two mile line running north-westwards from the town of Settle and across the watershed of the rivers Ribble and Eden to Carlisle. It was easy to draw a line Napoleonically across the map. Having done so the Midland's general manager James Allport, and engineer-in-chief, John Crossley, set off to walk the route, increasingly confident of their ability to build the line "until we got to that terrible place, Blea Moor".

IN the meantime, the London & North Western, becoming alarmed at the thought of the traffic which might be lost to a rival route to Scotland, made overtures of compromise to the Midland, offering improvements in connections and running rights over their route to Carlisle by way of Shap. Scarcely containing their joy at being let-off the construction and operation of a potential albatross, the Midland took steps to abandon their act, but they had not calculated the political implications of such a move. Victorian parliament was obsessed by the dread of monopoly. The country had already suffered badly at the hands of unscrupulous private railway companies with a monopoly of regional trade. The Midland was refused permission to abandon its Settle & Carlisle proposals and so, hoist by its own petard, the company reluctantly began to build the line.

"High stone walls, the colour of the succulent flesh of Solway sea trout . . ."

CARLISLE.

TO their credit the Midland set to its task with fists ready to pummel the Pennine wilderness, and no attempt was made to build the Settle & Carlisle on the cheap. The first sod was cut near Settle in November 1869. The company budgeted for a capital outlay of £2.2 million over 4 years of work. Five contracts were awarded; four for the main line, and one for the branchline to Hawes. A six thousand strong army of fighting, thieving, drinking and fornicating navvies was recruited along with a band of missionaries to curb their worse excesses. Temporary shanty towns were built along the course of the line to house the navvies, their families and camp followers. Somehow or other the men's energies were channeled for the most part into construction of the railway, though at no little cost to themselves; over two hundred of them died during the project.

GRADUALLY the semblance of a route began to take coherent shape. Viaducts hurled their mighty arches across ravines, tunnels penetrated the upper flanks of moorland. Where possible local materials were used.

HELLIFIELD. *"long canopies, like cathedral cloisters, reflect a lost importance . . ."*

ck blasted from a hillside was dressed on the spot by teams of masons then
sed, block upon block to span the adjoining valley. Spoil taken from cuttings
as tipped to build embankments, and if at first it slipped, it was tipped and
ped again. Four million tons of stone were used in the building of twenty
aducts and twelve tunnels. Progress was slow and the schedule slipped. In a
enario similar to the Channel Tunnel, the contractors went cap in hand to the
idland for more funds. At shareholders meetings questions were asked about
e viability of the project. Although limited mineral traffic was providing
:ome from the southern end of the line by 1873, the Midland could expect no
al benefits to accrue until completion of the through route. In the event, it took
ears and £3.5 million to complete the Settle & Carlisle. The first through goods
in ran on 2nd August 1875, but almost a year was to elapse before the stations
re completed and the line opened for passengers on 1st May 1876.

OR the next fifty years the Settle & Carlisle played a profitable and strategically
portant role in the fortunes of the Midland Railway. They advertised it as 'the
ost picturesque route to Scotland' and the Victorian and Edwardian travelling
blic took it to their hearts. The Midland introduced luxury Pullman
eping cars of
nerican design on
e route, and the
per classes of the
ome Counties, the
idlands and the
est Riding used it
quently and
thusiastically in
itation of the Royal
mily's predeliction
r Scottish holidays.
the turn of the
ntury Midland
presses were
vering the 112 miles
tween Leeds and
rlisle in 2½ hours;
nost too quickly for
ssengers
termined to enjoy
e line's scenic
tractions to the full.

were installed to cater for the vast amount of freight carried over the line. Even the
humble branch to Hawes carried heavy troop trains. In retrospect the war was a
watershed that the railways of Britain have never fully recovered from. The
extreme winter of 1947 saw the Settle & Carlisle's summit section closed for two
months because of snow drifts. Not a state of affairs, one suspects, that the
Midland directors would have been content to put up with.

NATIONALISATION of the railways took place on 1st January 1948. At
midnight the Midland whistles hooted mournfully across the moors. Overnight
control of the railway system transferred from the shareholders to the politicians,
and the general public were soon made to realise that nationalisation had simply
passed public transport from the frying pan of private monopoly into the fire of
politicial party dogma. No immediate change was apparent on the Settle &
Carlisle, gradually the line's best expresses regained their pre-war schedules, but
by the time Dr Beeching was made chairman of the British Railways board, there
were signs that the line was already regarded as a second rate route to Scotland,
and not in the same league as the East Coast and West Coast main lines. In 1963
the Beeching report recommended withdrawal of the Settle & Carlisle's stopping
trains but the
subsequent election of
a Labour government
the following year
caused this to be
postponed until 1970.

THE line's remaining
through passenger
trains and its still
relatively heavy
freight traffic led a
charmed existence
through the Seventies
but became an
obvious target for the
Serpell closure
proposals of the early
Eighties. This was to
be a cloak and dagger
decade for the Settle
& Carlisle. With
hindsight, British Rail

GARSDALE. *"Dales folk were devoutly chapel as opposed to church."*

HE Midland became part of the London, Midland & Scottish Railway in 1923.
perationally, little changed, apart from the developing use of more powerful
:omotives on the line. The Midland had preferred relatively small locomotives,
uble-heading where necessary. During the Thirties the LMS introduced a
ies of new locomotive designs, each more powerful than its predecessor, and
' 'Patriots', 'Jubilees' and 'Royal Scots' became familiar shapes on a line
herto the preserve of Midland 4-4-0 classes. In 1937 the Jubilee class
:omotive "Rooke" broke the two-hour barrier between Carlisle and Leeds
th a 300 ton test train.

JRING the Second World War the Settle & Carlisle was at its busiest ever and
 nation had cause to be grateful for the Midland's 19th century bravado. A
rd Anglo-Scottish route was vital to the war effort. Extra loops and sidings

can be seen to have been stacking the cards for closure from 1981 onwards. Even
such as revered a figure as Sir Peter Parker, the most obviously enthusiastic of BR
chairmen, has been accused of complicity in the skulduggery. The last vestiges of
the line's Scotch express service, already cut back from London to Nottingham,
were diverted away from the route amidst much controversy in 1982. They left
the Settle & Carlisle with a skeleton service operated by elderly and unreliable
locomotives and rolling stock calculated to deter all but the most determined
traveller. The motives were obvious and hackneyed: a vicious circle of
uncomfortable trains designed to create a down-spiral in revenue, resulting in a
cast-iron case for closure. Accusations of 'closure by stealth' hardly seemed
appropriate!

PASSENGER figures predictably nosedived, but then BR made a fatal error of
judgement. They appointed someone with a proven record in marketing to

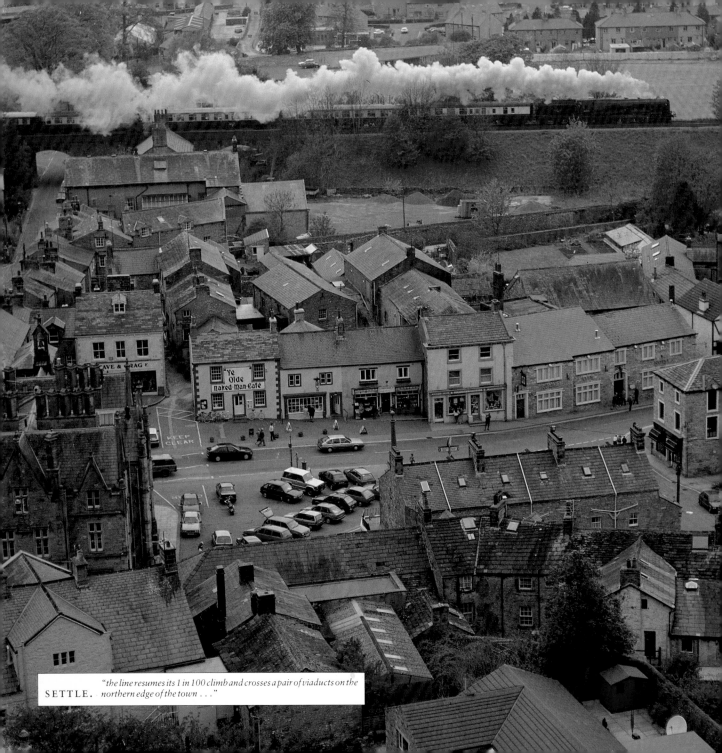

SETTLE. *"the line resumes its 1 in 100 climb and crosses a pair of viaducts on the northern edge of the town . . ."*

versee closure of the line, but at the same time maximising revenue. This Trojan Horse of a traffic manager, Ron Cotton, belonged to the 'pile them high, sell them cheap' creed and during his time at Liverpool had invented the extremely successful 'Saver' ticket. His appointment as project manager for the Settle & Carlisle can be seen now as an extraordinary *faux pas*. In many respects, however, his remit mirrored the impossibility of British Rail's overall, government inspired, ethos; the nationalised railway's eternal dilemma: is its function to provide the public with a social and environmentally kind service, or to maximise profits as an accountancy led activity? Ron Cotton's attempts to reconcile these often opposing goals encapsulate British Rail's conundrum as a whole.

BRITISH Rail issued formal notice of closure in December 1983. Opposition, at first surprisingly muted, grew as the decade wore on. Ultimately a record 22,500 objections were lodged. Travel figures increased steadily. British Rail claimed that these represented the emotional response of a public attracted by the controversy surrounding the line's closure and wishing to travel the Settle & Carlisle for a last time. Paradoxically, though, those who came for a final joy ride tended to be so taken with the experience that they came and came again and the railway's revenue mushroomed. In 1986 local authorities along the line sponsored re-opening of eight stations closed sixteen years earlier. Steam specials brought increasing publicity to the line, recreating the stirring scenes of the past, bringing back the sturdy beat of a locomotive working hard to master 'the Long Drag'.

YET in the face of this embarrassing success, British Rail were resolute in their determination to close the railway. They claimed that Ribblehead Viaduct was deteriorating and would cost £6 million to repair whilst use of the line came nowhere near to meeting this and other increasing costs. Many other issues ebbed and flowed against the future survival of the line and for its rescue. An option emerged for the sale of the line to a private buyer. The government encouraged this scheme, it encapsulated their dogma of self-sufficent public transport. But those in the know realised that privatisation of the Settle & Carlisle offered no simple panacea. BR would only be prepared to sell off a self-contained 72 mile route offering no direct access to Carlisle and Leeds, the traditional termini of the route. A private service restricted to the core section of the line was unlikely to be viable. In May 1988 the transport minister actually announced that he would consent to the closure of the line, but no firm date was given. Protests redoubled and figures were released to show that revenue had almost doubled during the Eighties.

IT would need a latter-day Gilbert and Sullivan to do justice to the imbroglio of the Settle & Carlisle during this time. Railway enthusiasts and supporters of public transport privately doubted if the line could survive the machinations of British Rail policy and the political intrigue. They braced themselves for the end of the line as they had done for the loss of numerous other rail routes down the years, imagining the line's great viaducts shorn of tracks, its tunnels sealed, its trackbed reverting to vegetation. They were not so much apathetic as disillusioned, there was scarcely any precedent for a railway closure being reversed by weight of public opinion. So it came as a great shock when the minister of state for transport announced in April 1989 that the government refused to consent to British Rail's closure proposal. No satisfactory explanation for such an astonishing volte-face has subsequently emerged, perhaps there were *tete a tetes* in the corridors of power, or late night phone calls taken in the panelled studies of country houses, but a hundred and

twenty-three years on, British Rail responded to being thwarted as admirably as the Midland had done. Indeed, they appeared magnanimous, joining with local authorities and other interested parties to produce a prospectus of 'Opportunities for Development' along the line, and introducing new 'Sprinter' trains along with an increased frequency timetable in the autumn of 1990.

AS the decade unfolds it will be interesting to see how services on the Settle & Carlisle are allowed to develop. The general public, if not railway enthusiasts, are said to appreciate the levels of comfort and reliability offered by the Sprinter trains with their welcome trolley-service of light refreshments, but the feeling has been voiced in some quarters that they are not ideally suited to the Settle & Carlisle service. Aesthetically, they are unable to emulate the virility of the Pennine landscape, as inappropriate as trying to do justice to Wagner with a snare drum and a tin whistle. Neither were the Sprinters, at first made up of three-car sets, thought to be capable of catering for the traditional surges of passengers travelling north from Leeds to see the Settle & Carlisle in the morning, and back from Carlisle at teatime. In May 1991, outside any clearly defined holiday period, passengers were having their ticket money refunded after being unable to board the already 'full and standing' 10.08 northbound service from Settle.

BRITISH Rail responded by strengthening the Sprinters into four-car formations, and by adding an additional 'Heritage' diesel multiple unit train at the height of the summer season, but remained adamant that they had no wish to reintroduce scheduled locomotive-hauled services. With '125' high speed trains being made redundant by the electrification of the East Coast Main Line it would be good to see a resumption of the classic St Pancras – Leeds – Carlisle – Glasgow/Edinburgh itinerary using one of these sets with dining facilities. But with British Rail divided into separate business centres by 'sectorisation', InterCity, whose aegis any such operation would come under, would probably be reluctant to incur the charges for use of the Regional Railways track between Leeds and Carlisle. On the other hand, privatisation of the railways may make the case for a daily, luxury service of this calibre more viable. Another obvious gap in the market is the lack of opportunity for people based in the north generally, and The Dales and West Riding specifically, to travel over the line by steam train. British Rail are aware of this and there is every chance that a more localised Settle & Carlisle steam operation may be introduced during the currency of this guide.

SOUTH of Settle, the tracks to Leeds have never suffered from the frequent identity crises experienced on the route to Carlisle. Commuter services between Leeds and Skipton are flourishing and due to be electrified by the middle of the decade, along with the branches to Bradford and Ilkley. New stations are earmarked in the Aire Valley and regular trains will probably be reintroduced on the Blackburn – Hellifield line at some point in the future, bringing the Settle & Carlisle within easy reach of the Greater Manchester conurbation. So it seems likely that England's most famous railway will continue to function and entertain us for the forseeable future. We hope that this guidebook will maximise your enjoyment of a journey along the line and exploration of its adjoining towns, villages and countryside. Everyone should travel the line once in their lifetime and thereafter not resist the temptation to make it habit-forming.

THE MOST INSPIRATIONAL railway ride in England begins at the least prepossessing of stations. Leeds 'City', is not, one suspects, an edifice which would appeal greatly to the architectural sensibilities of Prince Charles. It takes its cue from the industrial unit school of architecture prevalent at the time of its opening in 1967. But if the ambience is inauspicious, the trains themselves are positively contagious, and barely a moment seems to pass without one entering or leaving the station, bearing a destination label guaranteed to excite the imagination. Who could resist the charisma of Halifax, Doncaster or Goole? On platform 5 briefcase wielding businessman step nochalantly aboard the sleek 225 electrics to London King's Cross, but we are about to head geographically and metaphorically in the opposite direction and must content ourselves with the more ubiquitous upholstery of the Settle & Carlisle line 'Sprinter'.

"briefcase wielding businessman step nochalantly aboard the sleek 225 electrics to London King's Cross, but we are about to head geographically and metaphorically in the opposite direction"

These Sprinters, which constitute most Carlisle bound trains, and the more diminutive Metro 'Pacers' which form the Ilkley, Skipton and Morecambe trains, have the capacity to accelerate quickly, but complex pointwork and tight curves preclude a fast exit from Leeds station. Pulling out past Post Office red parcels vans stabled in the former Wellington station approaches, there are glimpses over the River Aire and parallel Leeds & Liverpool Canal, which accompany the line for much of its course through Airedale. Then, as the railway crosses the urban motorway in the vicinity of the old Holbeck station, you can look down on a former roundhouse engine shed and crescent-shaped repair shop dating from the dawn of the railway era; the former now finding use, not quite so romantically, as a depot for a van rental firm. Beyond, in amongst all the office blocks, are the University's Portland stone Parkinson building, the slender, golden-owl-topped spires of the Civic Hall and the tower of Cuthbert Broderick's magnificent town hall.

Overlooked by the castellated ramparts of Armley Gaol, the line burrows through deep cuttings of stone retaining walls, bearing the patina of soot left behind by generations of steam trains, past the site of Armley (Canal Road) station. This, along with other stops between Leeds and Shipley, was closed in 1965; though given the local authorities excellent record of re-opening stations some of them may grace the timetables yet again, especially as the programme of electrification gets underway. Certainly a station at Armley would be useful, for this is a busy industrial zone and a stop here would also be handy for Armley Mills Museum.

The line between Leeds and Shipley was opened by the Leeds & Bradford Railway company in 1846. The route had been surveyed by George Stephenson who favoured the easier, though longer course through the Aire Valley; 14 miles compared with 10 across the hills by way of Pudsey. The Midland Railway took over the Leeds & Bradford in 1851. During the remainder of the 19th century traffic grew, and steps were taken to widen the existing two tracks into four. Most of this quadrupling has reverted to double track once again, though loops for goods trains remain to the south of Kirkstall Junction signal box. But clues to former extra lines are readily apparent in the trackless bridge on the eastern side of the train as the railway crosses the canal between Armley and Kirkstall. The four lines were classed as 'up' and 'down', 'fast' and 'slow'; up and down being accepted railway terminology for the direction of travel, up, generally meaning in the direction of London. At Kirkstall a fly-over was built to carry the fast lines over the slow ones, but this, together with the adjoining power station, was demolished in 1967. From the western side of the train, you can catch a glimpse of the former power station canal basin where barges, with electrically inspired names like "Arc" and "Relay", unloaded cargoes of coal from as far away as Goole.

Kirkstall is another station which is likely to be re-opened and plugged into the admirable Metro system of local trains in West Yorkshire. There is a tantalising view, across the cabbage fields, of the ruined 12th century abbey. A Cistercian order came here from Fountains Abbey in 1152. The monastry was built from locally quarried stone and completed within thirty years. For nearly four centuries the monks went about their austere and silent routine until Henry VIII brought about the Dissolution. By the 18th century the abbey was no more than a romantic ruin, a source of inspiration for poets and painters alike. In contrast to the faded pomp of the abbey, Kirkstall Forge continues to thrive as part of the GKN group, producing axles for commercial motor vehicles. The forge dates back to the 17th century, and once had its own sidings, shunted by a saddle tank now preserved at the Middleton Railway Trust.

"There is a tantalising view, across the cabbage fields, of the ruined 12th century abbey."

The Aire meanders back and forth beneath the railway as the line passes the sites of former stations at Newlay and Calverley. The canal too, is a constant companion, and there are glimpses of two sets of hefty 'triple rise' locks as they set about the task of lifting the waterway up and over the Pennine chain. There's a 400 feet climb to be faced between Leeds Basin and the summit section of the canal at Barnoldswick. Hard work for today's pleasure boaters, but small beer to railway travellers bound for a thousand feet above sea level. With a milepost reading 202 miles – measured from the Midland Railway's London terminus, St Pancras – Apperley Junction is reached and the branch line to Ilkley diverges in a northerly direction.

Apperley Viaduct was swept away by the swollen waters of the Aire in 1866. The line then bridges the canal, at a point where once there was a rail connection into the huge sewage works at Esholt The works once had its own internal railway, at one time amounting to over 20 miles of track. Esholt village, about a mile to the north of the railway, is used as a film set for Yorkshire Television's everyday story of country folk, "Emmerdale Farm".

Between Apperley and Shipley the river curves northwards in a wide arc around a bluff of high ground. The canal followed suit, but the more technically advanced railway builders dug through the hillside and formed Thackley Tunnel, almost a mile long. A second tunnel was bored alongside when this section of the line was quadrupled in 1901, and this is the one in use today. The portals to the original bore, now disued, are visible at either end. On the far side of the tunnel the landscape will change perceptibly. Bare topped moorland will begin to rise like a monkish tonsure above the housing estates. Just quarter of an hour out from Leeds, and already the magic of this memorable railway journey is beginning to cast its spell.

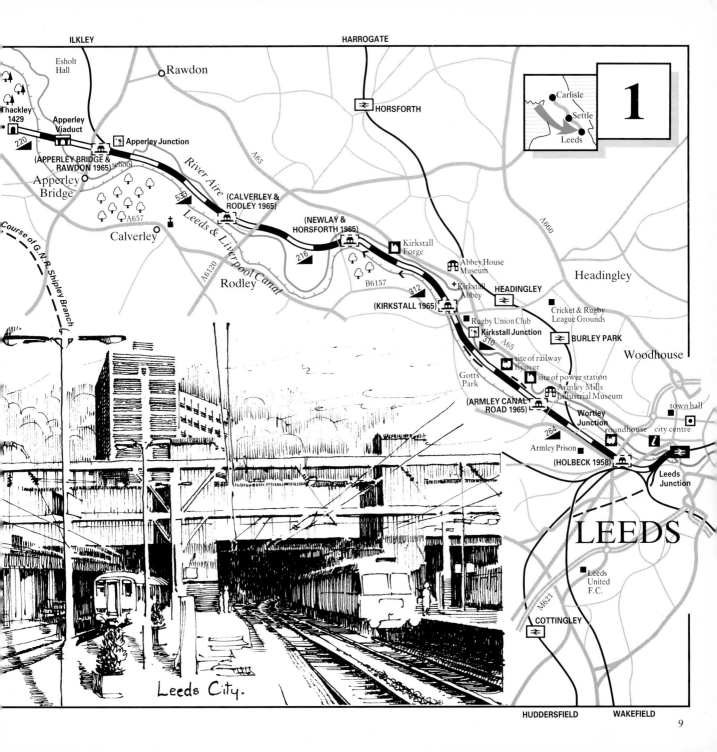

ILKLEY HARROGATE

Rawdon

Esholt
Hall

HORSFORTH

1

Carlisle

Settle

Leeds

Thackley
1429

220

Apperley
Viaduct

Apperley Junction

(APPERLEY BRIDGE &
RAWDON 1965) school

Apperley
Bridge

A657

River Aire

(CALVERLEY &
RODLEY 1965)

Calverley

A6120

538

A65

Leeds & Liverpool Canal

Rodley

216

(NEWLAY &
HORSFORTH 1965)

A660

Kirkstall
Forge

Abbey House
Museum

Headingley

B6157

312

Kirkstall
Abbey

HEADINGLEY

Cricket & Rugby
League Grounds

Woodhouse

(KIRKSTALL 1965)

Rugby Union Club

BURLEY PARK

Kirkstall Junction

370 A65

Course of G.N.R. Shipley Branch

site of railway
flyover

site of power station

Gotts
Park

Armley Mills
Industrial Museum

town hall

Wortley
Junction

264

roundhouse

city centre

(ARMLEY CANAL
ROAD 1965)

Armley Prison

(HOLBECK 1958)

Leeds
Junction

LEEDS

Leeds
United
F.C.

M621

COTTINGLEY

Leeds City.

HUDDERSFIELD WAKEFIELD

9

BETWEEN SHIPLEY AND KEIGHLEY the railway traverses a part of Airedale once dominated by the satanic mills of the textile industry. Cheek by jowl stand the mill towns of Shipley, Saltaire and Bingley, their factory chimneys punching the Pennine sky in a salute to Victorian energy and arrogance. But these often flamboyantly ornate perpendicular monuments to trade form a petrified forest now, and smoke no longer billows into the West Riding sky in a visual affirmation of a prosperity that has vanished. Nowadays the mills themselves house art studios, craft shops and all manner of small businesses, reminding you, in a way, of the peasants who colonised the great houses of the aristocracy after the Russian Revolution.

Once the line has emerged from the gloomy depths of Thackley Tunnel it is rejoined by the river and the canal. At Guiseley Junction the line to Bradford comes in from Ilkley under the watchful eye of a classic Midland Railway signal box. A set of mill buildings and a widening in the canal form a backdrop to the junction at a point where the old Bradford Canal passed beneath the railway. On the opposite side of the train you can see the former station building of the Great Northern Railway's branch line from Bradford by way of Idle. Prior to the grouping of 1923 – and even afterwards when the railways of the West Riding were divided between the L.M.S. and the L.N.E.R. – competition for passengers and goods was very real, though the Midland was obviously the winner here, for the Idle line lost its passenger service as early as 1931.

The Shipley triangle has nothing ostensibly in common with the Bermuda Triangle – though some long suffering commuters, waiting for trains which never materialise, may dispute this – but in railway terms the three converging routes form a fascinating layout. In truth Shipley did not become a completely triangular station until 1979, for up until then, no platform was provided on the main line. Historically the pattern of services was from Leeds to Bradford and Bradford to Skipton, the through traveller between the capital of the West Riding and the 'gateway to the Dales' usually being required to change at Shipley. When the emphasis changed, and services began running through between Leeds and Skipton, trains had to reverse into one of the platforms facing Bradford. And even when the main line platform was provided, only the down line one was built, forcing up trains heading for Leeds to cross on to the opposite track to call at Shipley. But if the complexities of the railway at Shipley are a headache for the railway operators, they provide much entertainment for the enthusiast, and the surviving station, with its obvious family resemblance to those at Bingley and Keighley, its cobbled approach road, handsome panneled booking hall, delicate ironwork, glazed urinals by J. Duckett & Son of Burnley, and its pair of pristine signal boxes, is a delight to explore.

Barely has the northbound train gathered speed from a stop at Shipley than the brakes go on for Saltaire. The station here was re-opened under the auspices of Metro in 1984, and when you get off the train – as really you should – you step not just on to the platform but back in time as well, for the whole village of Saltaire seems caught in a time warp, as though the twentieth century was just a bad dream from which you had awoken back into the more measured pace of the 1880s. Every attempt was made with the new station to perpetuate this illusion. There are imitation gas lamps, Midland look-alike diagonal fencing, flower baskets and trim stone waiting shelters unspoilt by graffiti. In short the station forms the perfect introduction to the astonishing model village of Saltaire whose abundant charms are catalogued in the gazetteer.

Reminders of Sir Titus Salt's paternalistic regard for his workforce are evident as the train passes sportsgrounds still bearing his name on the northern edge of the village. A mile beyond Saltaire the railway and the can cross the Aire at Dowley Gap, the latter by way of a stone aqueduct easily see from the train. Blocks of high-rise flats herald the approach to Bingley, and you pass through a short tunnel of 151 yards before entering the station. Sto built and substantial, with extensive canopies, the Midland obviously regarded this as a stop of some importance, though nowadays there is a slightly forlorn feel to the station, part of which is used by a dancing school rumbas and tangos where they once pasted labels on the left luggage. Beyo the station a sizeable goods shed – unconnected with the tracks now, of cour – can be seen on the down side, whilst opposite an attractive manual signal box remains in use. British Rail plan to modernise the signalling arrangemen between Leeds and Skipton at some point in the future, leaving the line to b controlled from a single power box at Leeds, and spelling an end to the romantic lever-frames and block bells housed in these neat timber cabins.

If it's winter, then a good proportion of your fellow passengers may be wearing underclothing made in the famous Damart works which overlook the railway just north of Bingley station. Ask your neighbour if they are, this The North, they won't be offended. Tucked alongside the works is a three-ri lock on the Leeds & Liverpool Canal. The better-known Bingley Five-Rise, one of the so-called 'Seven Wonders of the Waterways', is situated just beyond, though frustratingly less visible from the train.

Shipley – Bradford

Most travellers on the Leeds, Settle & Carlisle route chose to ignore the bran down from Shipley to Bradford, which is a shame because there is a lot of character – mostly, it must be admitted, of an industrial nature – in its three miles. Crossley & Evans's scrapyard at the outset sets the tone. This is one o only two sources of regular traffic for Railfreight between Leeds and Carlis Three days a week trains of scrap depart from here to steelworks at Rotherham and Sheerness in Kent. All these industries in Airedale, all those quarries up in limestone country, and it all gets jam-packed on the roads. Th scrapyard has its own diminutive shunting engine, the Hunslet built "Prince Wales". As the train slows for the only intermediate station, Frizinghall, yo can trace the course of the old Bradford Canal in the middle distance. In its prime it was reputedly so polluted that noxious gases burnt on its surface wit a blue flame. It was abandoned in 1922, the last regular trade being from th quarries up on the tops of Bolton Woods.

The Midland Railway's noble terminus at Forster Square was being demolished as this guide book was compiled. The long canopies reached ineffectually out along trackless platforms and the tiled entrance to the once exclusive Midland Hotel – designed by Trubshaw, the Midland Railway's chief architect – stood echoingly derelict. In place of the old station a modes modern structure of three platforms has been built to serve the city into the next century. The line from Shipley will be electrified and the direct service London will be increased. Indeed, there may even be through trains to the Continent via the Channel Tunnel, but one wonders if the new station will ever attract the same affection as its predecessor. Bradford folk held it dear t their hearts. It was their gateway to the holiday haunts of Morecambe Bay an the West Country. For many years the railways ran a special 'Residential' tra between Morecambe and Bradford for textile magnates senior enough not t have to reach the office before half past nine in the morning, and wealthy enough to live in comfort on the coast. The return train left shortly after five and combined with a portion from Leeds at Skipton. Apparently there was something of the atmosphere of a gentleman's club on board. Forster Square other famous train was 'The Devonian' serving Torquay and Paignton, an 8 hour journey to the seaside in the days of steam.

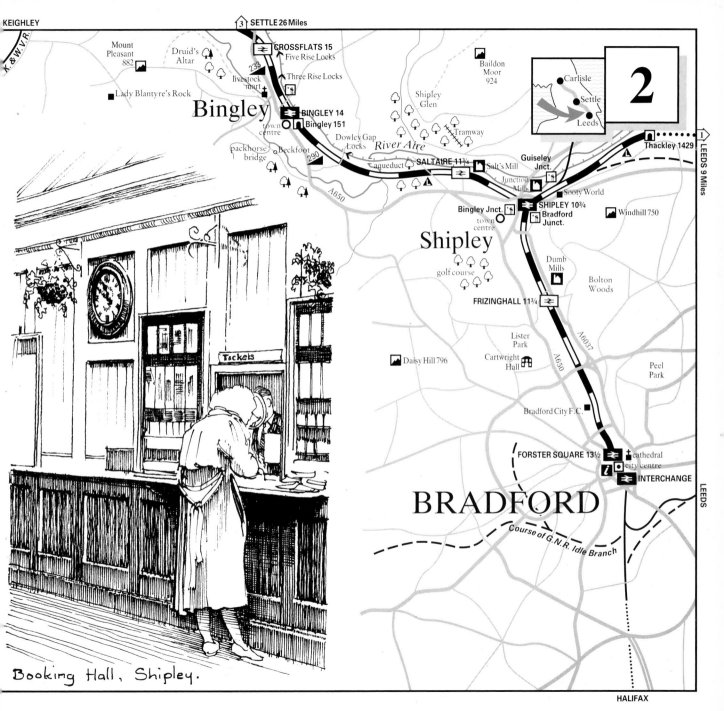

KEIGHLEY

K. & W. V. R.

SETTLE 26 Miles

3

Mount Pleasant 882

Druid's Altar

Lady Blantyre's Rock

CROSSFLATS 15
Five Rise Locks

233

Three Rise Locks

livestock mart

Bingley

town centre

BINGLEY 14
Bingley 151

packhorse bridge

Beckfoot

290

Dowley Gap Locks

River Aire

aqueduct

A650

SALTAIRE 11¾

Salt's Mill

Baildon Moor 924

Shipley Glen

Tramway

Guiseley Jnct.

Junction Mills

Bingley Jnct.
town centre

SHIPLEY 10¾
Bradford Junct.

Sooty World

Thackley 1429

LEEDS 9 Miles

1

2

Carlisle
Settle
Leeds

Windhill 750

Shipley

golf course

Dumb Mills

Bolton Woods

FRIZINGHALL 11¾

A6037

Daisy Hill 796

Lister Park

Cartwright Hall

A650

Peel Park

Bradford City F.C.

FORSTER SQUARE 13½

cathedral
city centre

INTERCHANGE

BRADFORD

LEEDS

Course of G.N.R. Idle Branch

HALIFAX

Booking Hall, Shipley.

Excursion No. 1 – Barging up to Bingley

Down in the bowels of Shipley, beyond the Salvation Army Citadel and the great locked gates of the old canal warehouses, lie the premises of Apollo Canal Carriers, operators of the Metro Waterbus service along the canal to Bingley. As bus services go, the timetable isn't frequent, and the schedule is slow – 1½ hours for 3 miles – but if your idea of a civilised speed is in the region of 4 miles an hour, then leave the train behind for a while and take to the unhurried waters of the Leeds & Liverpool Canal.

*   *   *

We caught the waterbus on a sunny May Day bank holiday, the sort of day when you dither about wearing a coat or not. In the event we needn't have worried; the day warmed up and stayed warm. The waterbus runs from Shipley to Bingley and there are intermediate stops at Saltaire, Hirst Wood and Dowley. Looking delightfully incongruous, bus-stop like signs hover over the pick-up points, and the public can board the boat at any stop as long as there is room on board. The secret, however – especially if you've come from afar – is to book in advance to make sure of your seats, otherwise you may be left disappointingly behind, a fate which befell quite a number of prospective passengers on this busy bank holiday.

Apollo usually use their 'narrow boat' of the same name on the waterbus run, the company's wide beam 'short boats' being allocated to the supper cruises and charter parties which are another aspect of the business. Managing Director, David Lowe, explained that *Apollo* is "a bit more zippy," and more suitable for keeping to the timetable than the larger vessels. *Apollo* looked in pristine condition, gleaming in the sunshine against the quay at Shipley Wharf, and we learnt that it had been built in 1929 as a horse-drawn boat, working on the Shropshire Union Canal between the Mersey Ports and the Black Country.

Excited passengers were now filling the hold where cargo had once been methodically stacked. Sharp on ten-thirty, a '*Queen Mary*' of a klaxon blarred, the ropes were cast off and *Apollo* chugged away from the wharf. The crew set about their separate tasks. Derek came through the boat checking tickets whilst Alan steered with the tiller at the stern. Following the *Marchioness* disaster, cruise boat operators – even on the placid waters of the canals – are particularly safety conscious, and a tape was played over the public address alerting passengers to possible hazards, especially when the boat is passing through locks.

Only a few minutes after leaving Shipley we were passing between the high canyons of the old mills at Saltaire. The towpath was busy with bank holiday crowds and quite a few people were waiting at the waterbus stop. We had room for just three of them, and Derek apologised to the rest, recommending them to try the afternoon service which hadn't been so heavily booked. They would have three hours to wait, but Saltaire isn't short of attractions: there are rowing boats to be hired on the Aire, or rides to be had on the famous cable tramway.

With Sir Titus Salt's ornate community church to 'port', we set off along the short reach to Hirst Lock. A lengthy excursion train snaked past us on the adjoining railway, and we were left making comparisons between the tortoise and hare of 19th century transport. As we approached the lock Derek jumped

ashore and ran forward to operate the sluices, or 'paddles' as they call them canal circles. The lock was half full and there was a fair amount of water to be released before one of the two, huge mitred gates could be opened for us to enter the chamber. Canal locks have been likened in principal to domestic baths. To fill them you turn on the taps, to empty you pull the plug. Derek had effectively 'pulled the plug' to empty the lock and now he swung the gate open to let us inside. Thud, the gate shut behind the boat, and for a moment it felt as though we were imprisoned in a watery dungeon. On either side of *Apollo* the sheer, slippery walls of the chamber rose dauntingly above us. Out of sight, Derek began 'turning on the taps' and as the water surged in we began to enjoy the sensation of rising in the chamber. Five minutes later *Apollo* had completed its ascent to the upper level and, after opening one of the lock gates to let us out, Derek went ahead to push the adjacent swingbridge open for us to pass through. All go, this canal travel, we thought!

More disappointed customers were turned away at Hirst's Mill, emphasising the wisdom of booking in advance. Alan spoke a few words of commentary as the boat threaded its way through the overhanging trees of Hirst Wood. He pointed out one of the old boundary stones of the Leeds & Liverpool Company and described how the horse-drawn boats of the past were worked day and night. Apollo themselves had carried the last cargo of coal along the canal to Skipton in 1980.

We wondered what the professional boatmen of the past would have made of this pleasure boat full of chattering tourists and all the people taking their leisure by walking along the towpath; all a far cry from the muck and brass images of the working past.

At the far end of the wood the canal is carried across the River Aire by way of a lengthy aqueduct. We had glimpsed its mellow stone arches from the train on several occasions, but the unusual experience of mixing these usually disparate elements of air and water was particularly thrilling.

Beyond the aqueduct the locks at Dowley Gap came into view. Here two locks are merged into one, lifting the canal almost twenty feet. The lock at Hirst Wood had seemed large enough, but Dowley Gap looked positively gargantuan. We had to wait for a pair of holiday hire boats to pass down the locks, an operation which took about a quarter of an hour. Not that time passed slowly: we sipped our drinks bought from the tiny bar at the back of the boat, and admired the well tended surroundings of the canal which had been awarded the best kept locks in the region by British Waterways in 1990.

In due course the other two boats emerged from the lock and there were waves and smiles on both sides. *Apollo* was nudged into the lock in front of an admiring audience of onlookers who obviously derived as much satisfaction as we did from our measured ascent. Derek, Alan and Gordon the lock-keeper kept up a tirade of good humoured banter which would stand them in good stead if they ever decided to swap the canals for a career as stand-up comedians. The sun shone, the boat gleamed, the water surged and the world looked pretty good from where we sat, three rows back from *Apollo's* bows.

There is another waterbus stop above the locks alongside the popular "Fisherman Inn". Once again we had to turn away potential custom. One lady entertained us all by going through the motions of diving in to the canal and swimming along in our wake. The pretty countryside which had bordered the canal since Saltaire began to be replaced by the urban periphery of Bingley. High rise flats loomed over the water and mills and factories lined its banks;

businesses which would once have relied upon its cargo carrying capacity in the commercial heyday of the Leeds & Liverpool. Our journey had covered a mere three of the hundred and twenty seven miles between the Yorkshire and Lancashire termini of the canal, but it had certainly given us an appetite to explore more of this fascinating canal, and we were looking forward to visiting it again when we researched one of the 'Walkabout' features at Gargrave.

Apollo was turned in the 'winding hole' at the foot of Bingley 'Three-Rise' locks in the shadow of Damart's well known thermal underwear factory. Earlier in the trip Alan had explained that a winding hole was old boatman's parlance for a turning point in the canal, and that the term had arisen from the habit of letting the wind blow the boat round in a specially widened part of the canal.

The waterbus stop at Bingley is right alongside the station. a good many of the passengers set off to walk the half mile up to the 'Five Rise' locks which lie beyond the regular route of the waterbus. But on this occasion we had a train to catch and, as *Apollo* departed on the run back ,we sauntered over to the station. It would take us just six minutes to get back to Shipley!

Information

Contact Apollo Canal Carriers Limited, Wharf Street, Shipley, West Yorks BD17 7DW – Tel: Bradford (0274) 595914 – for bookings and details of dates of operation and fares. Shipley Wharf is less than 5 minutes walk from Shipley railway station, whilst the waterbus stops at Saltaire and Bingley are even closer to their respective stations. Light refreshments are usually available on board the waterbus and there are numerous establishments en route, refer to the Gazetteer for more details.

"Apollo" at the locks, Dowley Gap.

NORTH of Crossflats the river is bridged again. Either side of the line ridges etched by stone walling rise to meet moorlands which, for the northbound traveller, anticipate the scenic splendours to come. A new dual-carriageway and a sewage works do what they can to spoil the view, whilst a pair of gasholders prevent all but a distant glimpse of the 17th century National Trust property of East Riddlesden Hall on the east bank of the river. In a moment or two the industry of Keighley will impinge, but there is every indication that the railway is beginning to escape from the conventional image of the West Riding and find its way out into the Broad Acres of another kind of Yorkshire altogether.

Like the old football cliche, Keighley is a station of 'two halfs'. The configuration is unusual – two separate pairs of platforms laid out in a shallow V shape. The British Rail side of the station has been refurbished, the roomy booking hall with its Midland seating and airy skylight taking pride of place. The other half of the station belongs to the Keighley & Worth Valley Railway, whose five mile branch line climbs assiduously out of this landscape of mills and foundries up into the resonant textures of Bronteland. So, at Keighley, the Sprinters and Pacers of the Nineties come face to face with steam locomotives and vintage carriages that are the images of childhood. Somewhere up in the Worth Valley, the Railway Children are eternally at play in the imagination of us all. And even if the Worth Valley local isn't waiting lazily at its platform, steam licking round its coupling rods, the lovingly kept station, with its posters vouchsaving the charms of long forgotten holiday resorts, hints at glories up the single line to Haworth and Oxenhope that are hard to resist.

The Aire Valley trains, however, make a quick getaway from Keighley, treating you to fleeting glimspes, barely retained, of textile works, dye factories, engineering plants and foundries: the lifeblood of the town, tens of thousands of livelihoods; all those people trying to keep the balls of their juggling act in the air while you swan supercilliously past on the train. Who was it who said that a journey is the ultimate escape from reality?

The line you are travelling on was promoted by the Leeds & Bradford Railway as an extension from Shipley to Colne. Skipton was reached in 1847, Colne the following year. As can be seen from the gradient indicators on the map opposite, this part of the Aire Valley offered fairly easy running. Flicking through the pages of old railway journals, the timing logs presented by the likes of Cecil J. Allen and O.S. Nock reveal that the steaming was easy on this stretch, and that the "Thames-Clyde Express" and "The Waverley" – London

to Glasgow and Edinburgh respectively – were easily capable of a 'mile a minute' along here.

Like a wing three-quarter who has spotted a likely opening, the railway makes for the Aire Gap. The sense of impetous multiplies, but there are still Metro halts to impede the progress of most trains. Steeton & Silsden was re opened in 1988. Just past the station Damart have another factory, and the you can see the huge Airedale Hospital on the same side. A mile further on t line crosses the boundary between West and North Yorkshire. Kildwick & Crosshills station closed in 1965 and hasn't as yet been rebuilt. The signal bo survives though, allowing the signalman to keep an eye on the busy level crossing which takes the A629 Skipton-Halifax road across the tracks. To th west you can see the chimney of an old lead mine on Gib Hill. To the east, sheltered by a mask of trees, stands Farnhill Hall, it dates from the 12th century and has four battlemented towers; defence against the border 'reivers', should they have chanced to maraude this far south. Just next to th house a typical hump-backed bridge marks the presence of the Leeds & Liverpool Canal.

Silsden.

Strangely, considering its rural setting, the station at the little village Cononley has joined the timetable again. Not that we should be anything but grateful, for Cononley is one of those enchanting wayside stations which seem almost to compel you to alight immediately from the train and melt into the landscape. Such qualitie are difficult to define, but you know them when you feel them. Here, perhaps, it is the simplicity which beguiles. Past the dignified Victorian mi a by-road curves to cross the Aire, beyon which looms the escarpment of Bradley Moor, topped by a cairn commemorati Queen Victoria's Jubilee of 1887. In the opposite direction the road winds through the village, ascends on to Cononley Moor, then swoops down in the loneliness of Lothersdale, threaded the Pennine Way. Once there were lead mines and iron ore quarries on the tops. is difficult to accept that Lancashire is only five miles to the west.

Seven minutes away stands Skipton. On either side of the valley floor hills begin to ride in waves on the horizon. The Aire, with built up banks, meander through the marshy terrain of Bradley Ings. The word ings is Yorkshire-spea for ground susceptible to flooding. Hereabouts the Aire has journeyed abou a dozen miles from its source at Malham and has another seventy to go to its confluence with the Ouse upstream of Goole. The adjoining hillsides, sprinkled with sturdy farms and patterned by drystone walls begin to have th look of The Dales about them; not the concerto or the symphony yet, perhap but the overture at least.

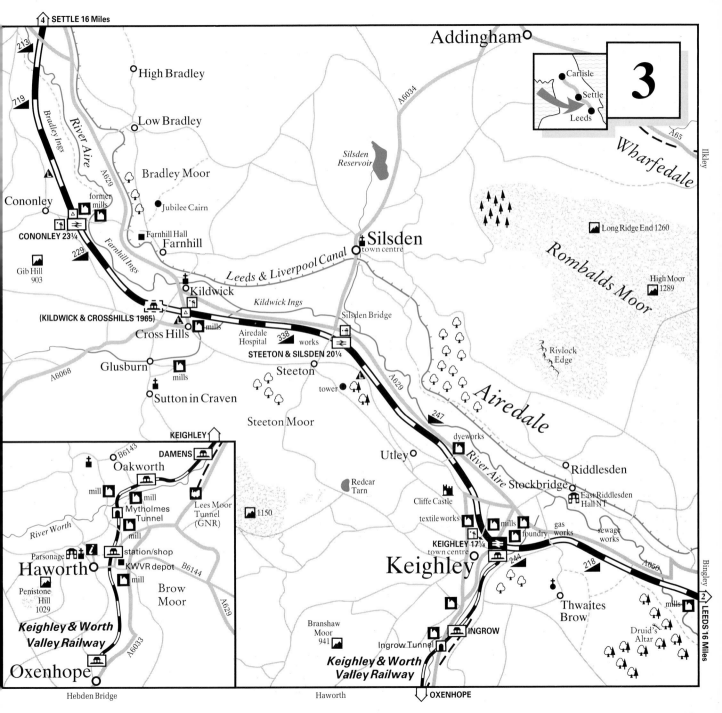

SETTLE 16 Miles

ADDINGHAM

Wharfedale

Carlisle
Settle
Leeds

3

Ilkley

A65

High Bradley

Low Bradley

Bradley Moor

Silsden Reservoir

Rombalds Moor

Long Ridge End 1260

River Aire

Bradley Ings

A629

Jubilee Cairn

Silsden
town centre

High Moor
1289

Cononley

former mills

Farnhill Hall

Farnhill

Leeds & Liverpool Canal

Rivlock Edge

CONONLEY 23¼

Gib Hill 903

Farnhill Ings

Kildwick Ings

Silsden Bridge

Airedale

Kildwick

(KILDWICK & CROSSHILLS 1965)

Cross Hills

mills

Airedale Hospital

338 works

STEETON & SILSDEN 20¼

A6068

Glusburn

mills

Steeton

Sutton in Craven

Steeton Moor

tower

A629

247

dyeworks

River Aire

Utley

Riddlesden

Stockbridge

East Riddlesden Hall NT

KEIGHLEY

B6143

DAMENS

Oakworth

Redcar Tarn

1150

Cliffe Castle

mill

Mytholmes Tunnel

Lees Moor Tunnel (GNR)

textile works

mills

foundry

gas works

sewage works

River Worth

mill

KEIGHLEY 17¼
town centre

244

218

A650

Bingley

Parsonage

station/shop

KWVR depot

B6144

Haworth

mill

Keighley

Brow Moor

Thwaites Brow

mills

LEEDS 16 Miles

Penistone Hill 1029

Druid's Altar

Keighley & Worth Valley Railway

A6033

Branshaw Moor 941

INGROW

Ingrow Tunnel

Oxenhope

Keighley & Worth Valley Railway

Hebden Bridge

Haworth

OXENHOPE

15

Excursion No.2 – In the Footsteps of the Railway Children

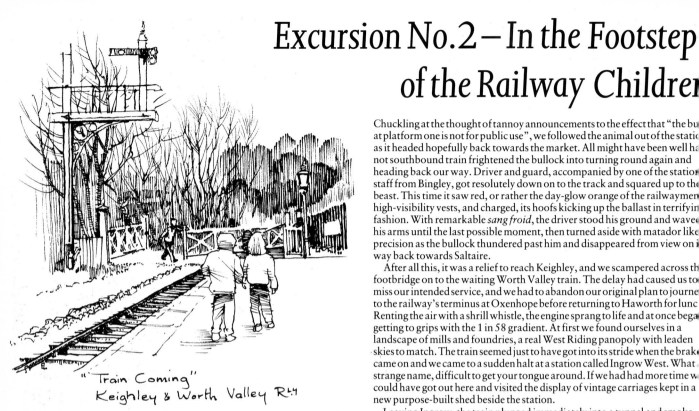

"Train Coming"
Keighley & Worth Valley R^ty

Chuckling at the thought of tannoy announcements to the effect that "the bu at platform one is not for public use", we followed the animal out of the stati as it headed hopefully back towards the market. All might have been well ha not southbound train frightened the bullock into turning round again and heading back our way. Driver and guard, accompanied by one of the statior staff from Bingley, got resolutely down on to the track and squared up to the beast. This time it saw red, or rather the day-glow orange of the railwymen high-visibility vests, and charged, its hoofs kicking up the ballast in terrifyin fashion. With remarkable *sang froid*, the driver stood his ground and wave his arms until the last possible moment, then turned aside with matador like precision as the bullock thundered past him and disappeared from view on i way back towards Saltaire.

After all this, it was a relief to reach Keighley, and we scampered across th footbridge on to the waiting Worth Valley train. The delay had caused us to miss our intended service, and we had to abandon our original plan to journe to the railway's terminus at Oxenhope before returning to Haworth for lunc Renting the air with a shrill whistle, the engine sprang to life and at once bega getting to grips with the 1 in 58 gradient. At first we found ourselves in a landscape of mills and foundries, a real West Riding panoply with leaden skies to match. The train seemed just to have got into its stride when the brak came on and we came to a sudden halt at a station called Ingrow West. What strange name, difficult to get your tongue around. If we had had more time w could have got out here and visited the display of vintage carriages kept in a new purpose-built shed beside the station.

Leaving Ingrow, the train plunged immediately into a tunnel and smoke billowed in from the open window; a smoke with the pervasive aroma of steam trains, which would sell in its millions if anyone ever got around to

Old Garsdale Turntable, Keighley.
Keighley & Worth Valley R^ty

THE adventures began before we even got to Keighley. At Shipley the guard, a genial Ulsterman, had come through the train and announced that we had been ordered to proceed cautiously because there was a cow loose on the line. Fortunately we were in the Pacer's front vestibule and had a good view through the door into the driver's cab of the line ahead. Trundling through the cutting to Saltaire we came upon the animal heading in our direction, trotting up the track in front of a Bradford bound train, like something out of a cartoon in "Punch". On close inspection it proved to be not so much a cow as thickset bullock with a determined look about him. From what we could gather he had escaped from the livestock market near Bingley station, three miles up the line. Our driver stopped the train and got down on to the track with the guard for moral support. Their presence was enough to turn the animal in his tracks and it set off back past the oncoming train and round the corner out of view. Our driver telephoned 'control' for further orders and then we rolled the few yards into Saltaire station where the passengers were still wearing the astonished look of people who had just *thought* they had seen a bullock walk past them up the tracks towards Bingley.

It took us three quarters of an hour to reach Bingley, not bad timing for a train travelling in the wake of a bovine. At Bingley, a sense of devilment appeared to come upon the animal, and it took to the platform, scattering passengers like onlookers at some Mediterranean bull baiting fiesta.

ttling the stuff. The next station along the line appeared to be called amens. We began to suspect that all the stops were made up of anagrams and ot real names at all. Oakworth brought us back into the realms of ausibility. This was the station which featured in the 1970 film of E. Nesbit's The Railway Children". Two of the most memorable incidents in the film, e landslide and the paperchase, were filmed at Mytholmes Tunnel just up e line from Oakworth. The little tank engine at the head of our train boured up the incline and was swallowed up in the darkness of the tunnel. hen the brakes went on for Haworth.

Haworth is the headquarters of the line where the railway's locomotives are stored and maintained. The station shop stocks an array of books and deos devoted to the many weird and wonderful corners of railway thusiasm. Some of us would have liked to browse here, but we were whisked vay over the footbridge and up the steep cobbled lane towards the centre of e village. Preconceptions are dangerous daydreams. If you arrive at aworth with cosy notions of the erudite Bronte sisters and their world being reserved in aspic you are quickly disillusioned by the touristy tinsel of Main reet. Here, if ever there was one, is the perfect, or should we say perfectly vful, example of a tourist haunt which has become the victim of its own iccess. Brash signwriting touted the attractions of each cafe, pub and craft op. People, just like us, with cameras, interpretive booklets and a betraying ck of purpose, mooched up and down the abrupt cobbled street like a crowd ene out of Disneyland.

We grabbed a quick sandwich from one of the ubiquitous cafes and decided walk back to Oakworth. Once the main street had been left behind, aworth regained some of its dignity, looking much like any West Riding mill llage snuggled in its own particular fold of the Pennines. In the distance we uld see the broad green back of Rombalds Moor. In the foreground lofty ill chimneys made vertical inroads into the weatherbeaten sky. As we turned to Mytholmes Lane we heard a whistle and saw cotton wool clouds of noke issuing from a train panting its way up the line. The children ran to tch a glimpse of it before it disappeared into the tunnel, and for a second or vo we were transmogrified towards the early years of the century and obby', 'Peter' and 'Phyllis' were scampering down the lane from 'High himneys' to wave to a passing train.

Crossing the river, we came upon one of the sizeable mills which still ariegate the valley, though few, if any, use the waters of the Worth as a power urce now or have any connection with the woollen industry. The road pped beneath one wing of the mill and then, a few hundred yards beyond, we ached the end terrace cottage where 'Perks' the porter lived with "the kids d the blooming Missus." Over the level crossing we went and into akworth station. The waiting room was deserted. A coal fire cast gleaming flections on the panelled walls. We half expected 'Perks' to bustle in from the cket office and pass the time of day. Outside on the platform the illusion was pheld by gaslamps, enamel signs, a trolley of milk churns and a barrow laden ith archaic cases and trunks: the sort of subtle attention to detail which laworth might do well to study.

ostscript.

alf an hour later we were whizzing back to Leeds and the last decade of the ventieth century. And do you know, they had only just caught up with the ullock. We saw him at Saltaire, pinnioned to the side of the track by three irly platelayers. The poor dumb beast looked exhausted. Heaven knows ow many times he had been up and down the line. We hoped fervently that a tter fate than the abattoir awaited him for his trouble.

Entering Mytholmes Tunnel, Keighley & Worth Valley Rly

Information

KEIGHLEY & WORTH VALLEY RAILWAY
Services run at weekends throughout the year and midweek in the high season. Talking timetable on (0535) 643629. General enquiries on (0535) 645214. When the railway isn't running an alternative method of reaching Haworth is by bus, and there are frequent services from Keighley bus station. Tel: Keighley (0535) 603284.

BRONTE PARSONAGE
Open daily. Tel: Keighley (0535) 642323. Place of pilgrimmage for avid Bronte readers. The family came to live here in 1820 and it remained their home for the rest of their extraordinary lives. Exhibits include manuscripts, letters and personal belongings. special events and exhibitions organised by the Bronte Society.

SET ON A graceful curve parenthasised by signal boxes, and retaining elegant canopies, Skipton station exudes a degree of charm, but is a pale shadow of its past. The useful lines to Ilkley and Colne have been lifted and the station cafe, which could be relied upon to provide sizeable fry-ups for hungry ramblers, has gone to that great refreshment room in the sky where Packed Meals of luncheon meat sandwiches and slabbed fruit cake still retail at half a crown.

At Skipton the line sheds a good proportion of its traffic, for this is the outer terminus of West Yorkshire commuterland, and the services which operate half-hourly from Leeds and hourly from Bradford go no further than this, except for a few extended along the line to Lancaster and Morecambe. Skipton is also the most northerly outpost for freight on the Leeds – Carlisle route. Trains of limestone aggregate, hauled for the most part by pairs of archaic class 31 diesels, run on behalf of the well known aggregates company, Tilcon, from Swinden Lime Works near the former Midland Railway branch terminus at Grassington, ten miles up the line. The railway connection keeps a tremendous amount of lorry numbers off the local roads and there are plans to increase the present schedule of six day and two night trains. The aggregates are delivered to Leeds for general use in the building industry, and to Hull for making tarmac.

"Dismantled railways exude a particular sadness and more often than not their loss seems such a waste."

The old Midland line between Skipton and Ilkley, closed in 1965, has risen pheonix like from its ashes to become privately operated as a tourist attraction by the Embsay Steam Railway. At present trains operate from Embsay station along a couple of miles of track in the direction of Bolton Abbey, a destination that the company hope to reach within the next five years or so. Bolton Abbey, and the neighbouring woodlands where the River Wharfe narrows to pass through 'The Strid', is a tourist attraction in its own right and re-opening of the station here would considerably boost the fortunes of the railway.

Though it has come down in the world, the station at Skipton is still worth perambulating if you have the time. The main up and down platforms are linked by a subway rather than a footbridge. This 'people tunnel' used to extend to a further pair of platforms provided for Ilkley line trains. The station buildings are executed in the same sort of soft creamy stone which travellers from the south have already seen throughout Airedale, but though the ticket office is manned, many of the rooms are empty now, and as you press your nose up against the window panes to see inside you can only conjecture as to their former use. Outside as you turn to look back on the station from the approach road, you discover the Midland's hallmark of a 'wyvern' still grimacing down from above the booking hall window.

The line northwards from Skipton was promoted by a company called the North Western and work began on the route in 1846. Railway Mania was at its height, and this modest outfit – who had nothing to do with the then recently formed giant, the London & North Western – had an eye on developing traffic between the West Riding and Scotland by linking Skipton with the Lancaster to Carlisle line. With hindsight the 'Little North Western' (as it became known in deference to the LNWR) was like a difficult piece in a jigsaw, a cause and effect with ramifications scarcely guessed at when the route was planned. Over the next twenty years the line became a battleground between the powerful Midland and London & North Western railways, and a

root cause in the Midland's eventual decision to build its own direct line to Scotland; the Settle & Carlisle.

Pulling away from Skipton you pass the former engine shed, now used as an industrial unit, and going under the by-pass, to the west you see the trackbed of the line to Colne threading its way disconsolately across the valley floor at the foot of Elsack Moor. Dismantled railways exude a particular sadness and more often than not their loss seems such a waste. The line from Skipton to Colne was closed in 1970, severing a through route between West Yorks and East Lancs which had stood for over 120 years. What act of book-keeping brilliance could justify such a closure? The respective stations at Skipton and Colne remain open, but the track between, just eleven miles of railway, has vanished.

Carlisle bound Sprinters make a rapid acceleration from Skipton and you soon emerge into a fresh landscape where mills are finally absent. With the Aire and the Leeds & Liverpool Canal keeping company with the railway there are views to the north-east of the forested flank of Sharp Haw and a hint of higher fells beyond. You are now in the Craven District of North Yorkshire an ancient name derived from the Celtic for 'land of the crags'. Gritstone has given way to limestone which outcrops like delicate lace trimmings on jade coloured lingerie. The A65 marks the western edge of the Yorkshire Dales National Park, but there's no need for such official recognition to appreciate the quality of the countryside. The station at Gargrave emphasises the change in origin of the railway which occured back at Skipton. The old booking hall, converted into a private residence, is charmingly, half-timbered and quite un Midland like in style.

A mile north of Gargrave the railway crosses canal and river in a sudden orgy of activity. You catch a glimpse of a lock on one side and the canal being carried over the Aire by aqueduct on the other. For a mile or two the river is on the western side of the line, and it indulges in an amazing sequence of tortuous meanders which, at one point, cause it to almost corkscrew itself. This turns out to be an elegant swansong, for at Bell Busk it says *au revoir* to northbound travellers and slips off in the direction of Malham beneath a graceful stone bridge. From the long closed station at Bell Busk a horse omnibus carried Victorian and Edwardian ramblers to the awe-inspiring scenes of Malham Cove and Gordale Scar which Turner, the landscape artist, had been inspired to paint earlier in the century. In 1951 Bell Busk station was used for scenes in an otherwise forgettable film "Another Man's Poison" starring Bette Davis.

"The landscape now is one of sensuously bare, rounded hills, the sort of slopes which in childhood you would have loved to go roly-poly down"

Between Bell Busk and Hellifield the railway crosses the low watershed of the Aire and the Ribble. Like a lottery, the becks that spring from the neighbouring moors find their way into one another of the rivers and subsequently, of course, into the North or Irish seas. The landscape now is one of sensuously bare, rounded hills, the sort of slopes which in childhood you would have loved to go roly-poly down until you were so dizzy you were sick. The pastures, dilienated by stone walls are still grazed by cattle, but their presence in the fields is becoming rarer as you head for the fells and sheep country.

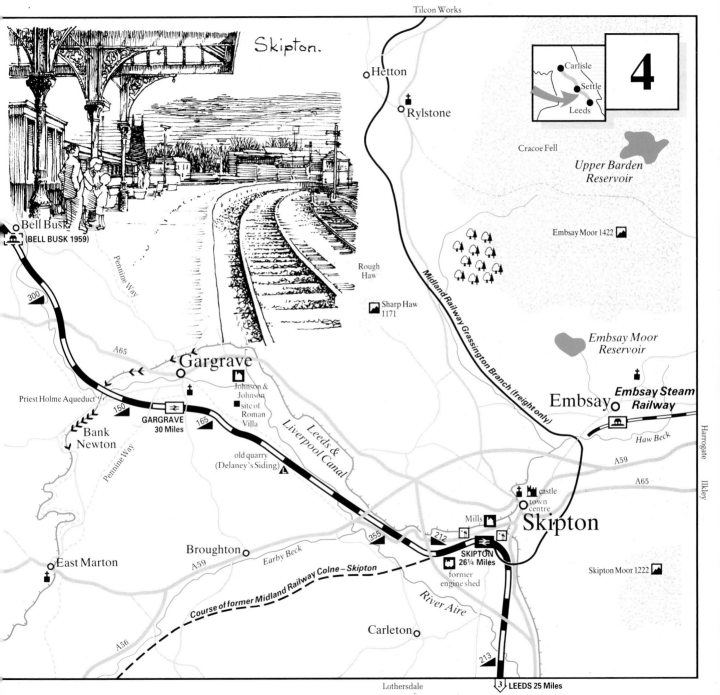

Skipton.

Tilcon Works

Hetton

✝ Rylstone

Cracoe Fell

4

Carlisle
Settle
Leeds

Upper Barden Reservoir

Embsay Moor 1422

Bell Busk
(BELL BUSK 1959)

Pennine Way

300

A65

Priest Holme Aqueduct

150

Bank Newton

Pennine Way

165

GARGRAVE
30 Miles

Gargrave

Johnson & Johnson
site of Roman Villa

old quarry
(Delaney's Siding)

Leeds & Liverpool Canal

Rough Haw

Sharp Haw 1171

Midland Railway Grassington Branch (freight only)

Embsay Moor Reservoir

Embsay   Embsay Steam Railway

Haw Beck

A59

Harrogate   Ilkley

A65

355

212

Mills

castle
town centre

Skipton

SKIPTON
26¼ Miles

former engine shed

Skipton Moor 1222

Broughton

A59   Earby Beck

Course of former Midland Railway Colne–Skipton

River Aire

East Marton

A56

Carleton

213

Lothersdale

3 LEEDS 25 Miles

19

Walkabout No. 1 – Roundabout Gargrave

The Pennine Way and the Leeds & Liverpool Canal are the stuff of inspiration for winter firesides. Map spread wide on the hearth rug, a circular route combining both suggested itself to us, beginning and ending at the Airedale village of Gargrave. Two months later, on a day holding the threat of rain, we walked down the road from Gargrave station, turning left almost opposite the church, on to the Pennine Way across the fields. A ditch at our feet was brimful with marsh marigold. Yellow waymarkers led us through the fields and over the railway to join a partially metalled lane divided by a strip of turf.

Nearing the farm which it serves, the lane divided and we bore left towards a prominent post on the brow of the hill. More stiles and waymarkers followed, taking us through pastures thick with the progeny of the lambing season. Our steps were dogged by larks and lapwings and a pair of curlews fluted across our heads. It became apparent that this was not the Pennine Way of the wilderness, but that of a gentler, almost ethereal agricultural England.

Presently the field paths gave way to a cinder track, but we were soon ba[ck] on grass, heading around the edge of a wood guarded, or once guarded, by broken down drystone wall dappled with lichen and moss. We passed a pair [of] well laden back-packers heading in the opposite direction, their brows firm[ly] fixed on Kirk Yetholm, and felt the guilt and envy of suburban commuters travelling between local stops on a far journeying express. Behind the mask [of] trees lay an abandoned quarry, perhaps used in the construction of the cana[l] which was now as close as it could ever be without revealing itself.

The path emerged from the field opposite a distasteful rubbish tip. We averted our eyes and marched along the lane towards East Marton. Below [us] on our right the canal threaded its way clandestinely through a ravine, fina[lly] betraying its presence with the staccato rhythm of a boat making its way towards Leeds. A few hundred yards later we came face to face with the cana[l] standing suddenly back as a farmer roared by on his 'quad' motorcycle wit[h] trailer in tow.

We turned in the direction of Liverpool and walked along the towpath to s[ee] the much photographed 'double-arch' bridge, an arch lain upon an arch wh[ere] the gradient of the original road was levelled out to meet the needs of mode[rn] traffic. Nearby stood a milepost indicating 89 miles to Liverpool and 38½ t[o] Leeds. We went up some steps to the A59 and met the modern traffic, a chastening experience which we soon put behind us, turning down the lane [to] the right beside the "Cross Keys Inn". The pub was shut, but any disappointment was quickly curtailed by the appearance of a cafe known quaintly as "Abbots Harbour" housed in a 12th century farmhouse of melti[ng] charm. Inside proved as delightful as out, and even at the outrageous hour [of] ten in the morning we availed ourselves of caramel gateau washed down wi[th] strong black coffee. A young farmer at one of the other tables was voicing t[he] need for rain, and not for the first time we appreciated the differing requirements of those who use the countryside for leisure and those who ma[ke] a living from it.

With a degree of reluctance we left the cafe and rejoined the canal, proceeding northwards back in the direction of Gargrave. Immediately the canal entered the rocky cutting we had sensed from the lane. We could see where the towpath had been sliced out of the underlying rock. On the far ban[k] ancient trees festooned an old quarry face. It was all so sylvan and silent no[w] but two hundred years ago it must have been a daunting section for the navv[ies] to tackle.

Emerging from the cutting, the canal found itself in a rolling landscape o[f] stone-walled pastures. Determined to avoid the need for locks, the canal builders had shaped it with the contours. What to our right had seemed like [a] second canal running almost parallel, was soon revealed as the Leeds & Liverpool winding ludicrously back on itself. A stone boundary wall and gnarled hawthorn bushes lined the towpath. The wind lapped the water up into wavelets. Rays of sunlight broke through the cloud to expose the dista[nt] line of fells, but we had become so disorientated by the zig-zagging canal th[at] we were hard put to name them. We wondered what the working bargeme[n] had made of the canal's lack of zeal to get anywhere fast. Had impatience giv[en] rise to Pennine blasphemy, or had they leant back on the tiller, chewed tobacco, and revelled in the glory of the passing scene? On one bend there wa[s] evidence of this lost trade, a post which had once held a vertical roller bar to ease the towing line round its sharp angle.

Leeds & Liverpool Canal, East Marton.

At Newton Grange we came upon a maintenance boat, its solitary incumbent busily engaged with the back page of a tabloid newspaper. Around the corner lay evidence of the canal surveyors reluctant admission of defeat by the landscape, the first of half a dozen locks taking the waterway down towards the Aire Valley. The towpath changed sides, and by the first lock we watched as an apparently inexperienced crew tussled with the unusual lock machinery, mouthing imprecations at each other drowned by the noise of the boat's engine. It occurred to us that boating holidays were not necessarily as peaceful and idyllic as they looked in the brochures.

As the long, grey holiday boat disappeared in the direction of Liverpool, its occupants still at odds, we continued down the flight of locks. A more expertly crewed yellow and blue boat was being eased through the third lock down. A pair of chattering girls went up the adjoining lane on ponies. The wind had carved more holes in the cloud and we could make out the moody, grey outline of Cracoe Fell beyond the jagged form of Sharp Haw. For a short distance the towpath became a road and changed sides, crossing a typical stone 'turnover' bridge of the sort which enabled boat horses to continue haulage without getting the rope strung over the parapet of the bridge. Cobbled setts snaked down to the towpath, and as we walked towards the neighbouring railway bridge a Sprinter wooshed by bound for Carlisle. Between the road and the railway the canal bridged the infant Aire by way of a graceful, three-arch aqueduct of simple dignity, and once again we enjoyed the thrill – experienced on the waterbus near Bingley – of water crossing water. Through the railway bridge stood a dredger called *Douglas*, smoke curling up from the cabin chimney while the crew were busily engaged reading the back pages of their tabloid newspapers.

Fostering illusions of a busy line, another Sprinter went by in the opposite direction and, passing through locks at well spaced intervals, the canal descended amiably into Gargrave. Past the "Anchor Inn" and under the A65 we went, skirting the parkland of Gargrave House, the dignified facade of which could be seen through a discreet mask of beech, ash and sycamore trees. School playing fields gave way to council housing with neat back gardens strung with washing lines. At Higherland Lock we said goodbye to the canal, which had entertained us so charmingly, and headed into the heart of the village.

Apple blossom was being blown on to the pavements. Dodging a shower we went into the "Dalesman Cafe" and had beans on toast amongst the chatter of cyclists stoking up with pie, peas and chips. We eavesdropped on boasts of distances covered and times achieved. Our own modest eight miles in three and a half hours couldn't compete, but we were not without a quiet, modest glow of satisfaction at the completion of our own small circuit of the Pennine Way and Leeds & Liverpool Canal.

The "Dalesman Cafe," Gargrave.

Information

DISTANCE & CONDITIONS
Start & finish at Gargrave station. OS Landranger Sheet 103. Eight miles, allow 3-4 hours net walking time. Conditions good.

REFRESHMENTS
CROSS KEYS – East Marton. Popular pub offering bar or restaurant meals. Theakston and Thwaites beers.
ABBOTS HARBOUR – East Marton. Delightful cafe and restaurant; also sells postcards, local books, confectionery etc.

Gargrave is well endowed with places to eat and drink and shop – refer to the Gazetteer.

WITH PENDLE HILL, legendary home of Lancashire's witches, prominent to the south-west, the train arrives at Hellifield, once a junction of some stature, though now a white elephant which no-one seems to want, or rather, can afford. Architecturally it is a gem, albeit a crumbling, corroding one which needs to be rescued soon if it is not to pass the point of no return. Its long canopies, which have been likened to cathedral cloisters, reflect a lost importance emphasised by the abandoned bay platforms where branchline trains once kept timetabled assignations with the Leeds – Carlisle expresses. The Lancashire & Yorkshire, sent its caramel slice coloured carriages up the Ribble Valley from Blackburn to fraternise with the florid crimson lake trains of the Midland and both companies had their own sidings, engine sheds and streets of employees housing here. Nowadays the only remnant of such importance is the group of porta-cabins occupied by the engineering department of British Rail, whilst, apart from maintenance trains, diversions, the Cumbrian Mountain Express steam specials and a limited summer Sunday passenger service, the Blackburn line is effectively unused. Officially BR and the local authorities and tourist boards would like to see Hellifield station developed as a heritage centre and interpretive point for the Settle & Carlisle line as a whole. But if such a scheme were to be privately sponsored the capital required would be colossal, and appropriate as such an idea might be – especially if Hellifield was once again a junction for passengers to and from the North West – there is no guarantee that it would be commercially viable. The profit motive was inherent in the origin of Hellifield as a railway centre, and it would need to be evident again for a renaissance to occur.

"The Lancashire & Yorkshire, sent its caramel slice coloured carriages up the Ribble Valley from Blackburn to fraternise with the florid crimson lake trains of the Midland"

To the north and east of the line the limestone fells that surround Malham become apparent. In contrast, to the west, the railway skirts the broad valley of the Ribble; its fields criss-crossed by a network of drystone walls which look somewhat out of place in so level a landscape. At the village of Long Preston, served (like Hellifield and Gargrave predominently by Lancaster and Morecambe trains) look out for the attractive row of almshouses known as 'Knowles Hospital'.

With the River Ribble and A65 main road in close attendance, the railway reaches Settle Junction; 40 miles and a bit out from Leeds, 234½ from St Pancras. Everything up to now has been no more than an *hors d'ouevre*. Airedale was fun, but it was no more than a taster for the main course which is upon you now. Here begins the line which you may well have travelled a long way to see. Rest assured that there is no anti-climax. Immediately the Settle & Carlisle starts climbing at its ruling gradient of 1 in 100 – see how the level Morecambe line appears to fall away to the west – and then becomes swallowed up in a rocky cutting of some depth. As you emerge from this the train loses speed on the approach to Settle station. To the east limestone outcrops rear up in a geological firework display of crags and caves and waterfalls.

The fact that you have arrived in mountaineering country is brought home to you by the steep drop necessary to reach the low platforms of Settle station. Steps are provided for the less agile, but a brave jump does seem an appropriate way to celebrate arrival at this lusty locale. Settle sets the tone for all the intermediate stations between here and Carlisle. Its style as been labelled 'Derby Gothic', a reference to the Midland Railway's headquarters and design centre. The Settle & Carlisle stations were built to a common style in three sizes. Settle, along with the other market towns of Kirkby Stephen and Appleby, is of the largest size. Though the style was common, the materials used were local; limestone and millstone grit between Settle and Kirkby Stephen, brick at Appleby, and sandstone through the Eden Valley. The stone used at Settle is said to have been quarried near Bradford. Perhaps the most unusual feature of the station buildings is that access to them can only be made from the platform side and not, as in most cases elsewhere, from the roadway as well.

Two delightful aspects of Settle station are the ornamental bargeboards decorating the gable ends, and the elegant screen fronting the entrance to the booking hall. The 236½ milepost from St Pancras is located at head height beside the screen at Settle. Towards the end of 1991 British Rail plan to install a footbridge to link the up and down platforms. The bridge is being brought in from Drem near Edinburgh, and though not of Midland Railway origin, it looks so much like the one at Appleby, that experts are beginning to think that bridges such as these were produced by an independent foundry as opposed to railway owned workshops.

In contrast with the main station buildings located on the up platform, the down platform is graced only by a simple waiting room. Beyond the boundary wall, part stone, part Midland pattern diagonal fencing, the land drops away into the valley of the Ribble, and then climbs again towards the neighbouring community of Giggleswick, dominated by the domed chapel of its famous public school, where the late Russell Harty taught for several years. In the foreground, hiding the river, stands the local creamery, and a former mill used for storage by a paper making company.

"To the east limestone outcrops rear up in a geological firework display of crags and caves and waterfalls."

Settle and Appleby are the only two stations between Skipton and Carlisle to retain their staff. Here the job of looking after the station belongs to Bob Smith, an Australian who, having heard that the position of leading railman at Settle was vacant, flew over from his home for the interview and landed the job. Settle is also the base for Paul Holden, Settle & Carlisle line manager whose job is to oversee the day to day running of the railway. It is apparently a labour of love, for Paul left a well paid job in the catering industry to escape the rat race and work closely with a line that he had known since childhood.

After a brief respite through the station, the line resumes its 1 in 100 climb and crosses a pair of viaducts on the northern edge of the town. The railway is already considerably higher than the river, which, between Settle and Langcliffe, has attracted a sudden flurry of mills. Though the Midland Railway's primary motive for building the Settle & Carlisle was for the Scottish traffic, a welcome revenue earning by-product was the development of several large lineside quarries. The first of these was opened by the Craven Lime Company at Stainforth in 1873. Its most notable feature was the massive 'Hoffman' limestone burning kiln which was topped by a 200ft high chimney Engine drivers would reputedly draw the chimney to the attention of young firemen, pointing out that the train had to climb to that height before it reached Ribblehead, and that they had better knuckle down and fill the firebox with coal. The former quarry is backed by Stainforth Scar, a dramatic rockface popular with local climbers.

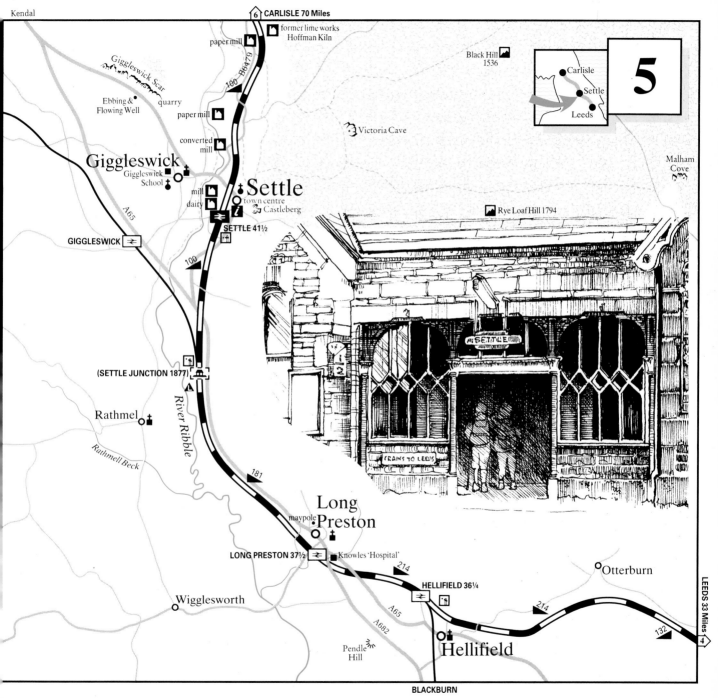

Kendal

6 **CARLISLE 70 Miles**

former lime works
Hoffman Kiln

paper mill

B6479

100

Giggleswick Scar

quarry

Ebbing &
Flowing Well

paper mill

Black Hill
1536

Victoria Cave

converted
mill

Giggleswick

Giggleswick
School

mill

Settle

dairy

town centre
Castleberg

Rye Loaf Hill 1794

SETTLE 41½

100

GIGGLESWICK

A65

(SETTLE JUNCTION 1877)

River Ribble

Rathmel

Rathmell Beck

181

**Long
Preston**

maypole

LONG PRESTON 37½

Knowles 'Hospital'

214

Otterburn

HELLIFIELD 36¼

A65

A682

214

132

Wigglesworth

Pendle
Hill

Hellifield

BLACKBURN

LEEDS 33 Miles

4

Carlisle

Settle

Leeds

5

Malham
Cove

Excursion No.3 – Cycling Round Ingleborough

INGLEBOROUGH is the one with the film star looks. Originally we had been going to climb it on foot from Horton station, descending from the summit by way of Gaping Gill and Clapham to the Morecambe line. But then this concept of a bicycle ride evolved as one of the featured excursions. For the sake of local research we hired our bikes in Settle, but could just as well have brought them there by train. Though if you do so, bear in mind that Sprinter trains are officially restricted as to the number of bicycles they can carry and space must be booked in advance*

*   *   *

Under an asbestos coloured sky we pedalled through Settle and out on the Horton road. The road runs parallel to the Ribble and is graced by old mills newly occupied as holiday flats and offices. We passed under the railway and turned into Langcliffe village to keep an appointment with a naked woman. Blazon hussy that she is, she sits high up on the wall of a house opposite the telephone box, though her modesty is preserved by the discreet positioning of her date of birth, 1660. Originally this house was an inn known as "The Naked Woman". Three years later those copycats down in Settle followed suit and opened an inn of their own called "The Naked Man". So much for the facts of life, the rest of Langcliffe is idyllic and it was tempting, this early in the ride, to go no further. We sat on the circular tree seat waiting for our 'second wind', listening to the trickle of the fountain commemorating the local men killed in the Great War; a piquant tribute, and we pictured them marching down the road to Settle station, never to return.

Reluctantly we returned to the B6479 and its convoy of aggregate lorries. Back over the railway and down past Robert's paper mill we free-wheeled. Seagulls were crying over the tip under Stainforth Scar, a melancholy and inappropriate noise so far inland. Over Stainforth Tunnel, past Taitlands Youth Hostel the road took us into Stainforth village where the pub is nicely named "The Craven Heifer". Out of the village by way of the Victorian church of St Peter we went and down the by-road to the ancient packhorse bridge which spans the Ribble. Proping our bikes against the parapet, we scrambled over the rocks to see Stainforth Force. The river spills over a series of ledges in picturesque style, then descends into a deep black pool said to be thirty feet or more deep. We thought it would be a wonderful spot for skinny-dipping, but doubted the wisdom of doing so.

Grateful for the mountain bikes' twenty-one gears, we made light work of the steep lane up to Knights Stainforth, turning right over Swarth Moor with the jagged outline of Smearsett Scar on our left-hand shoulder. Breasting the hill we were treated to a view right up Ribblesdale. Penyghent rose clearly above the valley but Ingleborough had its Hollywood head in the clouds. Downhill past the entrance to Dry Rigg quarry we continued, turning left on to the Austwick Road. Beyond the hamlet of Wharfe the road dips and we swooped down it, imagining ourselves with the yellow jersey, high up in the Pyrenees on the Tour de France.

The Old Viaduct, Ingleton.

Just short of Austwick we turned off the road on to a bridleway signposted 'Clapham 2 miles'. Our buttocks took a battering from the unfamiliar and uneven surface of the lane, but the sense of adventure increased proportionally to the discomfort. The map calls this Thwaite Lane, and having read somewhere that Edward Elgar and Dr Buck enjoyed walking it, we whistled, as tunefully as we could in the circumstances, a few bars of Pomp & Circumstance No.4. To our right stood Robin Proctor's Scar, somewhere beyond which lay the geological enigma of the erratic Norber Boulders.

The lane began to descend through mixed woodland. Peacocks were calling from the grounds of Ingleborough Hall, and a flock of ewes and lambs were being herded up the lane through the ornamental tunnels by a man in a Landrover. Clapham was gorgeous. A beck, which has travelled down off the south-eastern flank of Ingleborough, vanished into Gaping Gill and surfaced at Ingleborough Cave, bisects the main street, chuckling over its pebbly bed past the church and rows of delightful stone cottages which must be heaven to live in once you have come to terms with the tourists. There are plenty of cafes in the village, but on this damp Friday they all seemed to be shut. So we opted for a simple picnic from the village store and sat beside the beck watching the antics of a pair of wagtails, one pied, one grey, hopping from rock to rock in search of their own lunch.

It was four miles to Ingleton, the next stop on our itinerary, but the Italian 'Olmos' made mincemeat of the 1 in 7 out of Clapham, and were a revelation to us, brought up on Sturmey Archer 3 speeds. The scenery was pleasantly unspectacular, though were are fine views over the valley of the River Wennington up on to Burn Moor and the Forest of Bowland in the distance.

We pelted down the hill into Ingleton to find the market in full swing. Treating ourselves to cream teas in the "Copper Kettle", we bemoaned the fact that we couldn't walk across the old railway viaduct which spans the lower half of the town. This was going to be part of our pilgrimage, knowing how instrumental the 'end on' junction between the Midland and London & North Western railways here had been in the subsequent building of the Settle & Carlisle. The story goes that passengers were sometimes made to walk across the viaduct from one train to another, such was the animosity between the companies. With the viaduct having such historical importance, it seems ludicrous that the public cannot enjoy a walk across it; even if they had to pay for the privilege.

Ingleboro, from Chapel le Dale.

Disgruntled but not despondent, we took the lane to Twistleton out of Ingleton, and it turned out to be a botanist's dream. Even our inexpert eyes were able to identify primrose and bluebell, lady's smock and bugle. May blossom bedecked the dry-stone walls and peewits piped encouragement as we pummeled uphill. Ingleborough had shaken off its cap of cloud, revealing its handsome profile, dominant above the entrance to White Scar show cave. In the foreground the little River Greta twisted past stone barns and sheep filled pastures. To our left the screes of Twistleton Scar bordered the unfenced lane.

Inside the tiny church of St Leonard's at Chapel-le-Dale is a tablet stone commemorating those who died in the building of the railway between Settle and Dent Head. It is a nice way to be remembered. The low daylight cast a subtle glow through the stained glass windows. The congregation must be minimal, but the building and the churchyard are beautifully kept. We closed the door quietly behind us and passed through the lych gate, looking up at Ingleborough through a soft drizzle which had left a fine film of moisture our saddle tops.

Joining the old Roman Road from Ingleton to Hawes, we cycled past the "Old Hill Inn". Whernside was clear but the flat top of Ingleborough had vanished again. Ribblehead Viaduct, scaffolded like a cathedral tower, came into view as we breasted the hill. We pulled up for a moment to admire the view, tracing the course of the railway past the tiny speck of Blea Moor signal box, and following the line of tunnel spoil heaps and air shafts ascending the moor beyond. Amidst the evocative songs of the skylarks came the chatter of the workmen on the viaduct.

Ribblehead station was deserted. It reminded us of a wayside 'depot' in the sort of cowboy films they don't make anymore. A northbound Sprinter swanned haughtily by, but we rather treasure the absurdity of a station from which you can depart for the south but never return, or arrive from the north but never go back. A pair of chattering swallows were nesting in the eaves of the station building and a curlew flew over the tracks in the direction of the old Gearstones Inn where Charles Sharman stayed whilst overseeing the building of the line. From the platform we could keep an eye on all the Three Peaks and the hour's wait for the train back to Settle – which may have seemed interminable had this been Doncaster or Crewe – passed in the twinkling of an eye.

Information

BICYCLE HIRE – Mountain bikes are available from Settle Cycles (adjacent to the railway station – Tel: Settle (0729) 822216) and Castleberg Sports (Cheapside, opposite Town Hall – Tel: Settle 823751). If you are coming from far away we strongly advise you to book ahead with either company. At the time of writing charges were in the region of £12.50 per bike per day from 9am to 5.30pm; plenty of time in which to do the trip described (18 miles), or better still, one of your own devising.

*British Rail operate a bicycle reservation scheme on the Leeds – Carlisle route and, strictly speaking, carriage of a bicycle should be booked in advance (from any manned BR station or travel centre) for which a fee of £3 is payable. In practice, however, we have found that few guards would refuse to take a bicycle on board at one of the wayside stations along the line if reasonable space is available, bearing in mind the restricted luggage area on the Sprinter trains. The moral is book ahead to be on the safe side, but if you are staying locally you might risk it, after all you won't have too far to cycle back!

REFRESHMENTS
Clapham and Ingleton are well endowed with cafes, pubs and shops for picking up a picnic.

HORTON STATION. *"it is good to see signs of the station's horticultural reputation returning . . ."*

RIBBLEHEAD STATION. *"as though you were about to step off the planet . . ."*

INEXORABLY, the Settle & Carlisle continues its ascent towards Ribblehead, following closely the course of the river which spills and pitches downward over its rocky bed, seemingly in something of a hurry, to reach the Irish Sea. In the vicinity of Stainforth the valley narrows to almost gorge-like dimensions, and the railway encounters its first, albeit brief, tunnel. To pass through the gorge at its narrowest point, the railway engineers had to divert the river, which is crossed twice in only a few hundred yards. The B6479 shares the valley with the railway. A constant stream of quarry lorries use the road, carrying stone from the Horton area; a commodity which in a more sensible world would be carried by rail, to the general benefit of the environment. But lorry driving is a significant facet of the local economy, and it is doubtful whether the National Park authority have the commitment, still less the influence, to have this traffic transferred. Perhaps Malcolm Rifkind – if still Secretary of State for Transport by the time this appears in print – will bring pressure to bear on this irrational situation, now that the Government are openly espousing rail as an environmentally sympathetic transport mode.

Between Helwith Bridge and Horton-in-Ribblesdale the quarries line the western side of the railway. Three – Arcow, Dry Rigg and Horton – are currently in use; several others are worked-out scars on the face of the escarpment. Out in the open, the wind tends to play tricks with the sounds of the quarry machinery, teasing you into the belief that a steam train is labouring up the 'Long Drag', as this section of the line was known to footplate crews.

All the unstaffed stations between Settle and Carlisle are now looked after by representatives of the Friends of the Settle & Carlisle Line, but the group, following discussions with British Rail and other interested parties, have earmarked Horton for development as a 'heritage' station. Work has already begun on renovating the down platform waiting room, and in due course it is hoped that the main station building – currently used by permanent way staff – can refurbished and let for appropriate retail or commercial use. In the spring of 1991 British Rail issued a portfolio of architectural proposals to bring about a renaissance of the line. It considered the stations' fundamental role was to serve as a sequence of 'oases' in the landscape, attracting tourism to boost local economies without detriment to the environment. Ideally, funds permitting, all the station buildings would sooner or later be restored to their original condition: the stonework cleaned and protected, the windows renewed, and the interiors renovated as 'developers shells' for commercial lease. Where necessary, platforms are being extended to 102 metres – just over the length of a 4 car Sprinter unit – to comply with new Department of Transport regulations regarding the use of sliding door stock.

Platform heights will be raised as well. In happier times Horton won the Best Kept Station competition for seventeen years running and, following a period of decay, it is good to see signs of the station's horticultural reputation returning.

As northbound trains leave Horton, Penyghent can be seen broadside to the east. Penyghent means 'hill of the winds', and if you have made the ascent on anything other than a balmy summer day you won't be inclined to argue with that. Its limestone flanks are capped by an outcrop of millstone grit. The summit is 2,277 feet above sea level and is crossed by the route of the Pennine Way. Penyghent is one of a trio of famous mountains which dominate the Yorkshire Dales. The other two are Ingleborough and Whernside. Given suitable weather conditions, all of the 'Three Peaks' can be seen from the train. Ingleborough stands about three miles to the west of the line, slightly to the north of Penyghent. Both mountains, and indeed Whernside as well, can be reached on foot from Horton station. The greatest challenge to visit all of the Three Peaks in a day. The round trip is 24 miles long and can be done, if you are fit, in around 12 hours. The best fell runners in the annual Three Peaks Race manage it in 2½ hours!

If there is much enjoyment to be had on the surface of Three Peaks country, another sort of pleasure entirely can be derived from exploration of the underground world of caves and potholes which riddle this limestone landscape. Potholing – it goes without saying – is an activity for the experienced, but even the average rambler can gain a sense of the excitement involved by visiting some of the more spectacular 'pots' which form the entrance points to this subterranean world. Hull Pot, below Penyghent, and Alum Pot, above the hamlet of Selside, are two of the better known ones well worth going to see. The water which disappears into Alum Pot flows down Simon Fell, then emerges beside the Ribble at Turn Dub, to the east of the railway. For the less adventurously minded, there are show caves offering guided tours at Clapham and Ingleton.

Between Horton and Ribblehead the line climbs 200 feet in 5 miles. The landscape redoubles its sense of remoteness. Dwellings become few and far between, and you sense that the people who do live here have to be as hardy as the sheep which graze the drystone wall encompased pastures. Most of the walling was put up in the eighteenth century, prior to that Ribblesdale would have been an even more intimidating wilderness. Beneath the flanks of Simon Fell and Park Fell the isolated hamlet of Selside huddles under the railway embankment. The Midland Railway built two rows of employees cottages here which are still inhabited. They would have provided homes for the local signalmen and permanent way staff. Architecturally they echo the style of the station building along the line.

Midland houses, Horton.

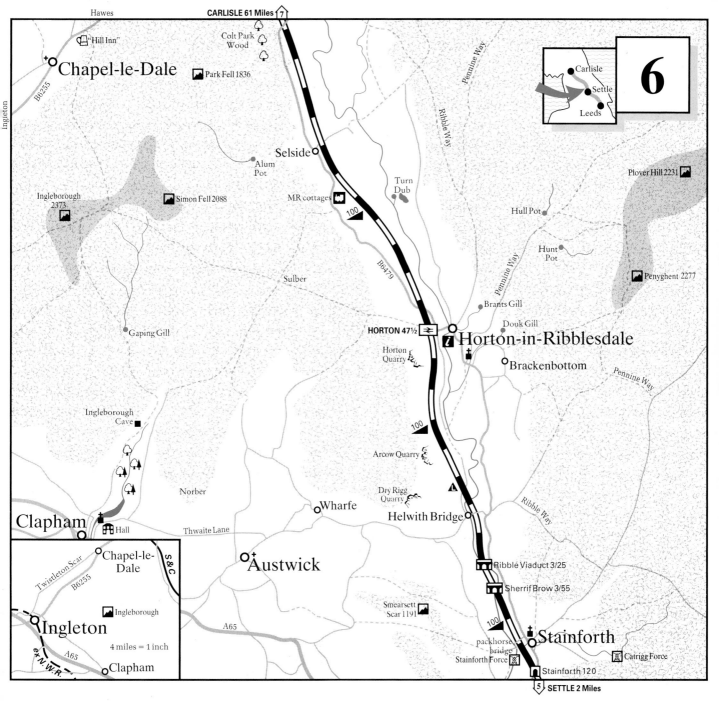

Hawes

"Hill Inn"

Chapel-le-Dale

B6255

Ingleton

Colt Park Wood

Park Fell 1836

Selside

Simon Fell 2088

Ingleborough 2373

Alum Pot

MR cottages

Turn Dub

B6479

Sulber

Gaping Gill

Ingleborough Cave

Norber

Thwaite Lane

Clapham

Hall

Wharfe

Austwick

A65

Pennine Way

Ribble Way

Plover Hill 2231

Hull Pot

Hunt Pot

Pennine Way

Penyghent 2277

Brants Gill

HORTON 47½

i Horton-in-Ribblesdale

Horton Quarry

Douk Gill

Brackenbottom

Pennine Way

100

Arcow Quarry

Dry Rigg Quarry

Helwith Bridge

Ribble Way

Smearsett Scar 1191

Ribble Viaduct 3/25

Sherrif Brow 3/55

100

packhorse bridge

Stainforth Force

Stainforth

Catrigg Force

Stainforth 120

6

Carlisle

Settle

Leeds

Twistleton Scar

S & C

Chapel-le-Dale

B6255

Ingleborough

Ingleton

4 miles = 1 inch

ex N.W.R.

A65

Clapham

Walkabout No. 2 – The Hill of the Winds

We took Wainwright with us the day we climbed to the top of Penyghent. Old 'AW' may be churning out his idiosyncratic, self-illustrated, hand-written books to more heavenly hills now, but there remains no better guide to the high places of Northern England. His book "Walks in Limestone Country" was first published in 1970. It has not been improved upon and is still in print. Within its charming pages thirty-four routes are described which would provide any Settle & Carlisle based visitor with plenty of inspiration for walks in the area. Walk No. 28 describes the route of the Three Peaks Walk from Horton-in-Ribblesdale to the summit of Penyghent, returning via the Pennine Way.

* * *

The Sprinter was echoing its way up to Ribblehead as we walked down past the old station-master's house, a sloping row of Midland Railway employees cottages, and across the Ribble into the centre of Horton. Had we been tackling the Three Peaks Walk – at 24 miles, a hard, full day in the fells – we could have 'clocked out' at the "Penyghent Cafe", a useful service by which tags can be kept on longer distance walkers to ensure they return safely at the end of the day. But at a modest six miles, the ascent of the local peak rarely presents walkers with serious difficulty. So we continued on past the cafe and called in at the village shop for chocolate bars, crisps and cartons of orange juice, modest sustenance for the climb ahead.

Beyond the shop we stayed on the main road until reaching the church, an ancient Norman building, standing picturesquely against the compelling backdrop of Penyghent. A man was mowing the graveyard. We thought of the christenings, marriages and funerals which had measured the lives of the village people down the centuries. A quarry lorry disturbed such daydreams, so we scurried away from the B6479, turning left up the first lane we came to, and soon afterwards crossing a footbridge over the adjoining beck. It was heartening then, to come upon a village school still functioning in these days of centralisation and that awful common denominator, the National Curriculum. We envied these tots their broad sward of mown grass with its tiny goalposts, and paused for a moment to listen to the chatter of childish voices from within the Victorian classroom.

The little road we were on began climbing gradually towards the hamlet of Brackenbottom and a goldcrest flew over the verge ahead of us. Half a mile from Horton a signpost pointed the way to the left across a series of stone-walled pastures in a more or less direct line towards the southern rampart of Penyghent. A soft drizzle had set in but the cloud cover was high. Only Whernside of the Three Peaks had its head in the mist. Sounds from the quarries on the opposite side of the valley mingled with the bleating of sheep around us.

Since Wainwright's day the Yorkshire Dales National Park have erected sections of raised timber walkway to combat erosion of the original path by the sheer volume of feet pounding up Penyghent. It's a popularity 'AW' couldn't have forseen, and if he could witness would shun. Popularising a particular place or landscape is the original sin of travel writers. Their enthusiasm to share their discoveries is sooner or later replaced by pangs of guilt at vulgarising them.

Penyghent - from Horton Church

Wainwright's meticulously drawn maps show the contours and altitudes of the landscape, and at 1700 feet we reached the southern edge of the peak. We took a breather and, resting on a pile of stones, watched a train beetle down the line past Helwith Bridge. In the distance to the south lay Pendle Hill, in the foreground an expanse of blotchy brown and green moor. We could trace the Pennine Way snaking its way over Fountains Fell and, here and there, an isolated farm eking out a precarious living in this often inhospitable setting.

With five hundred feet to go the gradient becomes more daunting. For the next section we needed to use our hands as well as our legs, and had to take care not to dislodge any loose stones on to the heads of fellow climbers below. We made diligent but exhilarating progress. Limestone gave way perceptibly to the darker gritstone, and although this climb is obviously child's play to any mountaineer, less exulted souls like us can derive much satisfaction from the ascent.

At 2100 feet the gradient eased and we approached the top upon a brow of moorland with more sections of walkway provided. It is necessary to admit to a niggling sense of anti-limax. A drystone wall runs across the summit, and looking north we might have been on any open stretch of moorland a thousand feet lower down. But there were little knots of backpackers noisily pleased with themselves, posing for snapshots by the Triangulation pillar, and their enthusiasm was infectious. By standing on the top of the stile which carries the Pennine Way across the neighbouring wall, we gave ourselves an extra few feet above sea level.

On the far side of the wall Penyghent lived up to the meaning of its name, and we faced into a cold north-westerly which hadn't been apparent on the southern side of the hill. Disappointing though the summit had seemed, the view now was intoxicating. To the north-east wave upon wave of fell reduced in density of tone towards the horizon, reminding us of those eerily featureless landscapes L.S. Lowry painted towards the end of his career. Looking north-west it is possible to make out Ribblehead Viaduct under Whernside and trace the seamless

Hunt Pot.

course of the Settle & Carlisle under Park Fell and Ingleborough. At around 1900 feet the path takes a right-angle turn to the west and becomes gravelled. We swung down the hill side at a spanking pace. This harsh 'white' path across the moor may appal the purists, but we could see already how confining walkers to this solid surface has done wonders for the surrounding flora. Various chuckling watercourses are heard making their first, infantile steps from the watershed down towards the Irish Sea. Crossing a stile over a drystone wall, we let Wainwright guide us to the left to see Hunt Pot, at which point one such watercourse disappears underground. 'AW' called this pot "an evil slit" and estimated that it is 200 feet deep. We dared not approach close enough to confirm or deny this.

Beyond the next drystone wall we turned right along the bridleway signposted 'Foxup' in order to visit Hull Pot, a more dramatic, though less deep chasm over which a waterfall pours after bouts of rain. Peering over the edge we could see primrose and lily of the valley growing tantalisingly on the rocky floor of the pot. Wainwright makes the interesting point that the streams falling into Hull and Hunt pots cross over themselves underground, emerging at Douk and Brants gills respectively, one of nature's intriguing sleights of hand.

We went bowling down the green lane to Horton, picturing ourselves as drovers of old with a flock of sheep for the siding at Horton station. A JCB digging in the garden of a house behind the village shop brought us down to earth and we repaired to the "Pen-Y-Ghent Cafe" where, understanding the needs of fell-walkers, they serve scalding tea in pint mugs.

Information

DISTANCE & CONDITIONS
Start and end at Horton station, OS 'Landranger' sheet 98. 7 miles, allow 3 hours net, conditions good but care needed on rocky, semi-vertical approach to summit.

REFRESHMENTS
Pubs, cafe and shop in the village of Horton – see gazetteer.

WHEN YOU STEP OFF the train at Ribblehead – and, at present, you have to be on a southbound train to do so – the rest of the passengers regard you impassively through their double-glazed windows as though you were about to step off the planet. Metaphorically, you are. An expanse of moor spreads itself beyond the station precincts like the mountains of the moon. Save for the welcoming pub at the foot of the station drive, signs of civilisation are conspicuously absent. A state of affairs which leads you to reflect that the station was an admirable choice for a weather station, a status conferred upon it in 1938. Stationmasters here received special training to carry out such unusual duties, after all they probably had more inches of rain to count than tickets to sell.

Nowadays Ribblehead is unique on British Rail in being only served by trains in one direction; southbound. Such an extraordinary state of affairs has nothing to do with rural depopulation, rather it is because the down platform was demolished, following closure of the station in 1970, to provide access to the since disused ballast sidings. When, fifteen years later, the line over Ribblehead Viaduct was singled, the lines were merged to the north of the station, no-one considering that the railway would remain operational much longer, let alone that Ribblehead station would soon re-open. So when it did, northbound trains had no platform to call at. However, now that the viaduct is being strengthened, British Rail hope eventually to re-double the track and once again provide a platform for down trains, putting an end to the eccentric anomaly of a station where passengers can leave for the south, but never come back! It has been suggested that Ribblehead may become an interpretive centre for the Settle & Carlisle. Passengers could alight here to visit the viaduct on foot, then tour an exhibition devoted to the construction of the railway housed in the renovated station building. Other attractions may include a museum of signaling where visitors could experience the feel of using a traditional signal cabin lever frame.

It goes without saying that Ribblehead Viaduct is the Settle & Carlisle's most potent and famous image. It spreads twenty-four colossal arches across the shakehole-strewn bog of Batty Moss, a name that in earlier days, and still on Ordnance Survey mapping, it bore. Statistics are meaningless in the presence of such grandeur, but for those who care for this sort of data the viaduct is a quarter of a mile long and over 100 feet high. In the Eighties it became the crux of British Rail's argument that the line would have to close. Cost cutting by the original 19th century contractors led to deterioration in the structure which British Rail, anxious in the early Eighties to find good cause to close the line, were only too hap   to present to the public and politicians alike as beyond economically viable repair. Wildcat figures amounting to several millions of pounds were banded about like stockmarket floatations, but, in the event, the viaduct has undergone a programme of repair at significantly less cost. Even now a latter-day shanty town of porta-cabins lies on the moorland floor beneath the viaduct where a hundred and twenty years ago the navvies toiled to erect this monument to the Midland Railway's ambition. In the summer of 1990 work began on repairs to the brick-lined arches and re-grouting of the piers. Trains slow to a crawl and passengers excitedly crane their necks to get a view of the curving viaduct in all its glory.

Batty Moss gives way to Blea Moor, the almost poetic resonance of such names matched only by the grandeur of the wild landscape. If and when the line across the viaduct is re-doubled, the LMS pattern signal box at Blea Moor may well close, bringing to an ambivalently regarded end a tradition of endurance going back to over a century. The signalmen here were as lonely as lighthouse keepers. In the past they lived beside the box, but nowadays they drive to Ribblehead and walk the rest of the way.

Overlooked by the eastern flank of Whernside, most northerly of the Three Peaks associated with the Settle & Carlisle, the line delves into cuttings before penetrating the southern portal of Blea Moor Tunnel. Almost one and half miles long, the Sprinters take only a couple of minutes to pass through the tunnel. In the old days, though the crew of a northbound steam goods might have to struggle for much longer to reach the other end in a nightmare journey of darkness and sulphurous suffocation. Blea Moor Tunnel was five years in the making. Seven shafts were sunk from the moor above, the extracted rock being winched up and deposited in a series of spoil tips on the surface of the moor. Three of the shafts were retained for ventilation, whilst the spoil, grassed over now, remains like a series of malignant growths on the swarthy surface of Blea Moor. When a steam special passes through the tunnel, smoke sometimes emerges in an eerie echo of the past from the air shafts which punctuate the sheep haunted landscape above the tunnel. The whole effect is stunningly surreal, and one wonders what Salvidor Dali might have made of it had he chanced to travel along the Settle & Carlisle.

The moorland above the northern portal of Blea Moor Tunnel has been planted, somewhat contentiously, with conifers. Traditionalists loathe the changed aspect brought to the once bare fells by such plantations, but those of us who come up here from a muted world of brown housing estates and grey motorways tend to be grateful for any hue and texture of green. Dashing out of the darkness of the tunnel the line finds itself at the head of Dentdale. Two precipitous chasms cleft into the fleshy hips of Wold and Dent fells are bridged by a pair of viaducts, Dent Head and Arten Gill, which, though they can't match the imposing length of Ribblehead, if anything are couched in an even more dramatic setting.

Passengers on the western side of the train are treated to an incomparable prospect of Dentdale, now part of Cumbria but once, more appropriately, of the West Riding. Far below the River Dee winds down the valley over a succession of limestone steps, beneath which it is apt to disappear during spells of dry weather, accompanied by a by-road which is part of the Dales Way, an 84 mile long distance path leading from Ilkley to Windermere. The hamlet of Stone House was once the site of a marble quarry. Arten Gill viaduct was built from this peculiarly coloured local rock, a darkish grey coloured limestone streaked with the patterns of white fossils. A mile beyond Arten Gill comes Dent station, and there is every temptation to alight here to explore the dale and the distant village of Dent.

Dent occupies a niche in the railway record books, for at 1,139 feet above sea level it is regarded as the highest station on a main line – if the Settle & Carlisle can still be so regarded – in England. It is 5 miles from, and 600 feet above, the village it purports to serve; though, to the sturdy inhabitants of Dentdale, well used to ascending on to the fell to dig for coal, this obviously posed no problem. The stationmaster's house is thought to have been one of the first domestic buildings in Britain to be double-glazed; the walls were also slated on three sides! Additional emphasis of the inclement location of the railway was the provision of two lines of snow fences to the east of the line. In practice, though, they were said to be more successful in providing cover for the sheep than keeping much snow off the track. But they remain to this day, grotesquely eroded, like a derelict groyne on an exposed beach. Just south of the station stands a rather nodescript single storey building which is thought to have been an original 'navvies bothy' dating from the construction of the line. The station building is in private hands now, and in the process of being refurbished for residential use. Shelter for train users is provided on the up platform, a welcome retreat whilst waiting for the train at the end of a hard day hoofing in the fells.

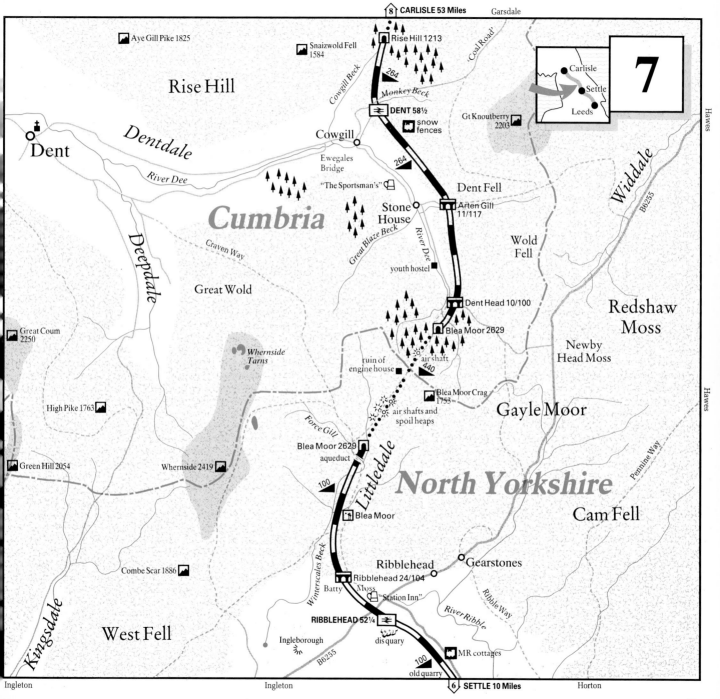

8 CARLISLE 53 Miles   Garsdale

Aye Gill Pike 1825

Snaizwold Fell 1584

Rise Hill 1213

Rise Hill

264

Monkey Beck

'Coal Road'

Cowgill Beck

Dentdale

Gt Knoutberry 2203

Dent

River Dee

Cowgill

Ewegales Bridge

"The Sportsman's"

264

DENT 58½

snow fences

7

Carlisle
Settle
Leeds

Hawes

Cumbria

Stone House

Great Blaze Beck

Dent Fell

Arten Gill 11/117

Wold Fell

Widdale

B6255

Craven Way

Great Wold

Deepdale

River Dee

youth hostel

Dent Head 10/100

Redshaw Moss

Great Coum 2250

Whernside Tarns

ruin of engine house

air shaft

Blea Moor 2629

440

Newby Head Moss

High Pike 1763

Blea Moor Crag 1753

Gayle Moor

Green Hill 2054

Whernside 2419

air shafts and spoil heaps

Littledale

North Yorkshire

Force Gill

Blea Moor 2629 aqueduct

Cam Fell

Pennine Way

Combe Scar 1886

100

Blea Moor

Kingsdale

Winterscales Beck

Ribblehead

Gearstones

Ribblehead 24/104

Batty Moss

"Station Inn"

River Ribble

Ribble Way

West Fell

RIBBLEHEAD 52¼

Ingleborough

dis quary

B6255

100

old quarry

MR cottages

Ingleton   Ingleton   **6** SETTLE 10 Miles   Horton   Hawes

33

Walkabout No.3 – Blea Moor in the Mist

Six people and two dogs stepped down from the early morning train at Ribblehead. Visibility was minimal. Crossing the viaduct had been like coming through the clouds on a descending jet. But up here you take your chances with the weather. Not risks, you understand, but chances, yes! We planned to walk back to the station at Dent, across the top of Blea Moor. This is arguably the definitive Settle & Carlisle linear walk, and it offers you the chance to appreciate three of the line's greatest viaducts and its longest tunnel in the context of their wild moorland setting.

Down the station drive we swung, past the still curtains-drawn pub, over the cattle grid and left along the track towards the viaduct. Campers were coming to terms with the dawn; stirring in their tents or grimacing through the condensation covering the windows of their mini vans. Enjoying the sense of superiority prevalent in people who have stolen a march on the rest of humanity, we felt our way towards the viaduct, and although it was impossible to see more than four arches at a time, there was a strange solemn beauty about the high arches in their shroud, reminding us of that line in Van Morrison's song about "the viaducts of my dreams."

Keeping close to the piers, we reached the north end of the viaduct and scrambled up the slope to where the path over the moor becomes more clearly defined. The National Parks authority have struggled to keep the 'Three Peaks' path from suffering total erosion, such is the quantity of feet pounding its surface into a miry waste. But hardcore is being put down to good effect without compromising the wide open spaces too much, and, as if to emphasise the popularity of the path, a party of back-packers came into view as we headed towards the signal box. Such passing platoons are ships in the night to the lonely signalman isolated in his remote box. In summer people must be passing him all day long, but he has to remain aloof, concentrating on his vital role. Out through his window he can watch the clouds cast moving shadows over Whernside, and listen to the lark between the tinkling of the block token bell. Beside the box stands the empty shell of one of two houses which once formed a railway worker's community here. It is no longer in railway ownership, and for some time an estate agent's For Sale sign has been optimistically displayed. But with no mains services and no access road one would need the outlook of the Savage in Huxley's "Brave New World" to counterance living in it.

A farmer was making his way across the moor by 'quad' with hay for his sheep as we left the box behind. The path began to deteriorate and there was a certain amount of judicious stepping over stoney becks and boggy bits to be done. A more clearly defined track veered off to our right. It was obviously the easiest route to follow, but was not marked as a right of way on the Ordnance Survey map. The authorised path runs close to the railway until reaching a peculiar bridge, half footpath, half aqueduct, which the railway engineers built to divert the waters of Force Gill across the line. Not far away Force Gill tumbles over an impressive waterfall as the 'Three Peaks' path begins to climb over the north-eastern flank of Whernside.

On the far side of the bridge a signpost points to Dentdale. We struck right towards the southern portal of Blea Moor Tunnel, past a second signpost indicating 2½ miles to Dent Head. Magically the mist began to thin. Brush strokes of pellucid blue daubed the sky. Out of the opaque distance strange mounds like giant molehills appeared ahead on the rising surface of the moor. Of course we knew that these were the spoil heaps of rock lifted to the surface when the tunnel was dug, but somehow that knowledge couldn't detract from the powerful mystery of the scene in front of us. For a moment we stood and imagined the activity here in the 1870s; the men, the machinery, the teams of horses and donkeys struggling through the mud, the sudden subterranean explosions of dynamite. Some direct descendents of the navvies were working on one of the air shafts. A century later and the need for maintenance goes on.

As we reached the top of the moor the mist engulfed us again, but the track was well trodden enough to be obvious. A couple of walkers passed us in the opposite direction and we commiserated with each other over the lack of views. We crossed a style and the path began to descend towards a third air shaft. The story goes that a local woman saw what she thought were enemy parachutists landing on Blea Moor in the early days of the second world war. The Home Guard were summoned, only to find that the 'parachutes' she had seen were pockets of mushroom shaped smoke hanging over the air shafts of the tunnel. The path grew steeper and passed through a conifer plantation, beyond which lay the northern portal of the tunnel. More banks of spoil stood adjacent to the track. A small beck passed beneath the line and tumbled over a waterfall. We crossed a footbridge over the beck and followed the track towards a derelict farm. The whitewashed farmhouse regarded us reproachfully as we crossed the yard, a sad commentary on rural depopulation.

Tunnel Airshaft, Blea Moor.

Dent Head viaduct loomed imperiously out of the mist like so many cathedral naves joined together. For the first time since leaving Ribblehead we were back in the world of motor cars, but there weren't enough of them to spoil the enjoyment of walking beside the little River Dee whose waters were trundling over its peculiarly formed bed of marbled rock. At Stone House we turned right up the lane to get a better view of Arten Gill Viaduct, surely the line's most dramatic, a choice for the connoisseur of viaducts as opposed to the more obviously popular appeal of Ribblehead.

Had the weather been kinder we would have followed the eroded track uphill beneath the viaduct on to Dent Fell, and found our way round to Dent along the old drover's road. But in the circumstances it seemed less than worthwhile to take the longer way round when the views would be restricted to the laces of our walking boots. In any case, half a mile along the road lay the tempting hospitality of "The Sportsmans", one of three pubs in Dent Dale dispensing the local ale brewed at Cow Gill.

Suitably fortified, we gathered our strength for the ascent to Dent station. Crossing the bridge at Cow Gill we caught a glimpse of the white breast of a dipper on the riverbank. We turned right by the old West Riding signpost. Twenty minutes of hamstring agony later, we puffed and panted our way into the station yard. Three youths formed a reception party. "We hoped someone would turn up," they beamed, "do you mind taking a picture of us next to the highest main line station sign?"

Dent Station.

Information

DISTANCE & CONDITIONS
Start from Ribblehead station, return from Dent*. OS Landranger sheet 98. Seven miles (10 miles via Arten Gill and Galloway Gate) allow 3½ or 5 hours respectively. Conditions largely good underfoot.

REFRESHMENTS
Pubs at Ribblehead and Stone House (Dent), see Gazeteer. No shops.

*Remember that at present only southbound trains call at Ribblehead station. Passengers from the south may find it easier to do this walk in the opposite direction to that which is described. Book to Dent, walk back to Ribblehead and pick up your homeward train there.

RISE HILL TUNNEL, second only to Blea Moor in terms of length, takes the northbound train from Dentdale into Garsdale; a valley watered by the River Clough, a tributary of the Lancaster Lune. At the western end of Garsdale stands the town of Sedbergh, something of a border post between the Dales and the Lakes, and best known for its public school. In the days of steam, water troughs were fitted between the rails between Rise Hill and Garsdale so as to enable express trains to pick up water without needing to stop.

Garsdale is bereft of any focal community, being rather a series of hamlets interspersed by lonely farms. The reason that there is any railway station here at all is because this was formerly the junction for the Wensleydale market town of Hawes. For many years the station was actually known as Hawes Junction. Thinly disguised as 'Gloam' in J.B. Priestley's early novel, "Adam in Moonshine", it was here that Adam Stewart detrained at the beginning of his picaresque adventures in 'Runnerdale' as the plot thickened to return a Stewart to the throne. So much for royalty fiction, but royalty fact has it that the Prince of Wales uses Garsdale station once in a while on his way up to the grouse moors.

The single track branchline to Hawes was six miles long and the train took around a dozen minutes to reach there before proceeding along North Eastern Railway tracks to Northallerton, forty miles and an hour and three-quarters away. Most of the trains were worked by North Eastern rolling stock and, by all accounts, it was a journey of spellbinding loveliness, which a local group are campaigning to revive. The track through Wensleydale remains intact and used by goods trains as far as Redmire, but an eighteen mile gap between there and Garsdale needs to be filled before passenger trains might once again run the length of this lovely dale. In the meantime a bus service links Garsdale station with Hawes, its setting down point being, appropriately enough, the old station yard, where the Midland Railway buildings have a new role as a Tourist Information Centre and Dales Museum. The section of line between Garsdale and Hawes closed in 1959, its trackbed is clearly visible curving away to the east of the main line as the train leaves Garsdale; another of those sad scars on the landscape which break the heart of those who feel that the only proper sort of wheel is one that has a flange.

It may not have been much of a population centre, but as far as the Midland Railway was concerned, Garsdale was perhaps the most significant station on the line. It had been intended that a locomotive depot be provided here, but in the event facilities were limited to a water crane and a turntable. The turntable entered railway folklore one night when a locomotive on it was caught by the wind and spun out of control, round and round and round, until someone had the presence of mind to pour sand on the moving parts, thus bringing the whole contraption to a shuddering halt. To avoid being similarly embarrassed again a pallisade of old railway sleepers was built up around the turntable to act as a windbreak. By coincidence, the deck from Garsdale turntable has found a new lease of life at Keighley on the Worth Valley Railway, and is visible from the BR line.

Sixteen company houses were built for the staff at Garsdale. It was a tight-knit community, living like Hebridean islanders surrounded by a sea of unremitting moorland. Their pleasures were simple. The water tank doubled as a dance hall and cinema, church services were held in one of the waiting rooms, and in another room there was a staff library of over two hundred volumes, donated by two regular lady passengers. Old photographs reveal how pretty the station looked. An extended canopy sheltered the 'island' platform at whose outer face stood the Wensleydale branch trains, patiently awaiting the next connection on the main line. Nowadays Garsdale, having closed in 1970 and re-opened in 1986, is looked after by members of 'The

Friends', but their enthusiasm can only make cosmetic improvements in the face of years of neglect. The signalbox remains intact but deserted like the *Marie Celeste* , several levers of its frame pulled permanently off so that the signals in the vicinity are always up. After the train has gone the silence is absolute. A tinkling beck magnifies voices from houses in the valley below and the clouds make patterns of light and shade on the haunch of Baugh Fell. In fact, the box may get a new lease of life if the line is re-doubled over Ribblehead Viaduct. When that has been done Blea Moor and Kirkby Stephen boxes will close and Garsdale will re-open as the only intermediate box between Settle Junction and Appleby.

Pulling away from Garsdale the train passes a disconsolate rank of sidings – there are no wagons to shunt for Hawes now – and then moves on to Moorcock Viaduct which carries the line across Dandry Mire. The engineers had planned to build an embankment across the mire but all the earth they tipped just sank into the bog. They carried on tipping for two years of Victorian stubborness before the penny dropped. On the roadside to the west, just as the line crosses the Sedbergh-Hawes road, stands the tiny Hawes Junction Methodist Chapel. Dales folk, in common with others whose lives were lived at the sharp end of existence, were devoutly chapel as opposed to church.

Another row of employees cottages can be seen to the east, together with the "Moorcock Inn", as the line curves towards a short tunnel named after the inn. This is followed by Lunds Viaduct, scene of bad accident on Christmas Eve, 1910. Two light engines which had banked trains up to Ais Gill and travelled on to Garsdale to turn, were waiting for a clear road back to Carlisle. Forgetting their presence, the signalman pulled off the signals for a St Pancras – Glasgow express, but the drivers of the banking engines took this to mean that they could proceed and trundled off at an ambling gait across Moorcock Viaduct and through the tunnel towards Lunds. The express, travelling at 65 miles an hour, caught up with them on the far side of Lunds Viaduct and the gas lit carriages exploded into fire as a result of the collision. Twelve people died, several of whom were buried in the churchyard at Hawes.

Ais Gill is one of the great British railway summits, its name belongs in the same hall of fame as Shap, Beattock, Talerddig, Dainton and Druimuachdar. Here, twenty-three miles from Settle and forty-nine from Carlisle, the line has reached the ridge tiles of its climb, 1169ft above sea level. It can be a turbulent, desolate place, overlooked by Wild Boar Fell on one side and the watershed of the Ure and Eden rivers on the other. The Midland Railway provided sidings here for slow trains to be stored or for banking engines to be detached. From the eastern side of the train you catch a glimpse of Hell Gill waterfall; strange that the origin of Eden should be in Hell.

Nearby the road from Garsdale to Kirkby Stephen crosses the line. It was here that an accident, similar in many respects to that at Lunds, occurred in 1913. On the night of September 2nd two sleeping car expresses were making their way up to Ais Gill, the first having left Carlisle quarter of an hour before the second. By virtue of its weight, the front train should have been double-headed, but a shortage of locomotives had led to it departing from Carlisle without a pilot. Furthermore the tenders of the locomotives on both trains had been filled with a batch of inferior coal and both drivers were experiencing difficulty on the climb to Ais Gill. In fact, the first, and heavier train stalled just short of the summit, whilst the following train passed through several adverse signals while its crew were preoccupied with coaxing their locomotive up the incline. In a ghastly repitition of the events at Lunds, the inevitable happened and the second train plunged into the rear of the first. This time there were eighteen fatalities.

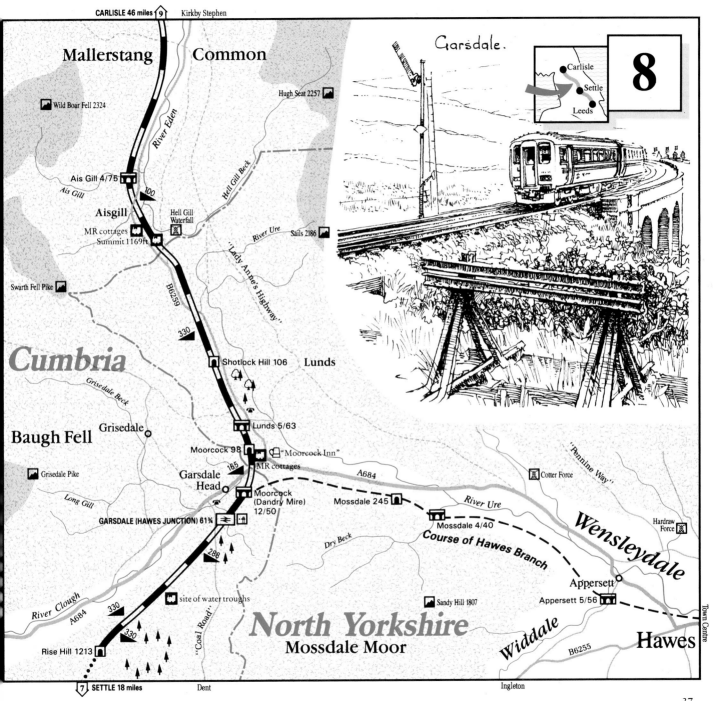

Kirkby Stephen

Garsdale.

8

Carlisle
Settle
Leeds

Mallerstang   Common

Hugh Seat 2257

Wild Boar Fell 2324

River Eden

Hell Gill Beck

Ais Gill 4/75

100

Ais Gill

River Ure   Sails 2186

Aisgill

Hell Gill
Waterfall

MR cottages
Summit 1169ft

B6259

330

"Lady Anne's Highway"

Swarth Fell Pike

Cumbria

Griesdale Beck

Shotlock Hill 106   **Lunds**

Baugh Fell   Griesdale

Lunds 5/63

Moorcock 98

"Moorcock Inn"

Griesdale Pike

Garsdale
Head

165

MR cottages

Cotter Force   "Pennine Way"

Long Gill

Moorcock
(Dandry Mire)
12/50

A684

Mossdale 245

River Ure

Wensleydale

GARSDALE (HAWES JUNCTION) 61¾

Dry Beck

Mossdale 4/40

Hardraw
Force

Course of Hawes Branch

288

Appersett

River Clough

A684

site of water troughs

Sandy Hill 1807

Appersett 5/56

330

330

"Coal Road"

North Yorkshire

Mossdale Moor

Widdale

B6255

Hawes

Town Centre

Rise Hill 1213

Dent   Ingleton

DENT HEAD VIADUCT, & WHERNSIDE. *"those of us who come up here from a muted world of housing estates and motorways tend to be grateful for any hue and texture of green."*

MALLERSTANG COMMON. *"tucked under the hem of Little Fell the line descends at the ruling gradient of 1 in 100 . . .".*

Excursion No. 4 – Market Day in Wensleydale

The branchline railway from Garsdale to Hawes closed in 1959. It had never been heavily used. By tradition, Hawes folk looked east along Wensleydale to Northallerton when they wanted anything to do with the outside world. One useful train, nicknamed 'The Bonnyface', left Hawes for Bradford in the afternoon, but is said to have carried more cheese than people. For the next thirty years Garsdale and Hawes might have been as far apart as John O' Groats and Lands End. Recently, though, local authorities have recognised the value of a link between the increasingly popular Settle & Carlisle line and the market town of Hawes, and have sponsored a bus service which meets the trains and brings visitors into the town, six miles from the head of Wensleydale.

*　　　　　*　　　　　*

Tuesday is the day to see Hawes at its best. It's market day and the little town comes to life as Dales folk gather for the weekly ritual of shopping and gossip. The livestock mart takes place as well, and the narrow cobbled streets of the town reverberate to the toing and froing of Landrovers, tractors and trailers. In summer the bus operates each weekday and meets several arrivals at Garsdale automatically; in winter it only runs provisionally on Tuesdays and Saturdays and you have to make sure by booking ahead. On the misty January morning that we made the trip we were the only passengers off the train, but this gave us the opportunity to chat with the friendly bus driver, and by the time we reached Hawes we felt we had learned far more about the town and its dale than we would have done by working our way through reams of well-meaning Tourist Board literature.

At the isolated "Moorcock Inn" we turned off the road to Hawes. The driver – who we had now got to know as Raymond – had to pick up an elderly lady from Lunds, a remote hamlet perched half-way up a hillside near the source of the Ure, the river which flows through Wensleydale before finding its way out into the North Sea by way of the Ouse and the Humber. We picked the lady up at the entrance to a driveway in the middle of a conifer plantation. She had braved the cold and walked down from Lunds to meet the bus. Raymond told us that there had been a Youth Hostel at the end of the drive, but that it had closed through lack of custom. Considering its setting, the grey expanse of moor and the dearth of other dwellings, we were not surprised. Lunds had also boasted an Anglican chapel, but it hasn't been used for years. "They're a heathen lot up here," laughed Raymond, and the old lady chuckled approvingly with the same wide smile which must have graced her face as a girl.

Back on the main road we kept close company with the old trackbed of the Hawes branchline, catching sight of the top of a tunnel it passed through and a graceful viaduct as well. At Appersett the road zig-zagged attractively across a couple becks and then we had to stop while a flock of geese waddled nonchalantly across the road. Despite the mist we could make out the pale outlines of Staggs Fell on one side of the bus and Widdale Fell on the other. On a sunny day the views must be intoxicating.

Twenty minutes after leaving Garsdale we arrived at Hawes. The bus dropped us, appropriately enough, in the old station yard. All the station buildings are intact and instantly recognisable as having been of Settle & Carlisle parentage. Ironically, the buildings are in a better state of repair than most of those on the line itself, because they house the local National Park offices, the Tourist Information Centre and, in the former goods shed, the Dales Countryside Museum. You can even get bed & breakfast in the old station master's house.

Because of the restricted winter service we only had a couple of hours to spend in Hawes, so we quickly set off to explore the town and see the sights. We didn't have far to go for our first port of call. Outhwaites have been making ropes in Hawes since 1905, and the business is still flourishing. A wide variety of ropes are made using a traditional ropewalk and visitors are welcome to pop in and watch the process and to look around the adjoining craft shop. The firm's colourful dog leads caught our eye and we bought one for our 'pooch', who had been forced to stay at home on this trip.

Hawes.

Coming out of the ropeworks, we saw a small van loaded to the gunnels with sheep, and followed it round to the cattle market, four or five hundred yards up the road. Sheep are still the most important facet of Dales farming, but on this occasion there seemed to be more cattle in the pens than ewes or tups. We were told that the main sheep sales aren't held until later in the year after the lambing. The whole place was bursting with farming folk, many of whom seemed to be there more for a natter than with any thought of doing business. The market itself would have made a fine setting for an episode of "All Creatures Great and Small" and, in fact, Askrigg, a village where much of the television series was filmed, is only a mile or two down the dale.

We wandered back towards the town, browsing in shop windows, admiring the irregular street pattern, the waterfall plunging beneath Hawes Bridge, and the way the church tower protrudes above the rooftops of the higgledy-piggledy houses. Hawes knows how to cater for visitors, but it also retains its integrity as a working town. The main employee is the cheese factory. We bought a pound of local Wensleydale wrapped in muslin from Elijah Allen's excellent shop in the Market Place. At the newsagents next door we picked up a useful 'town trail' leaflet. Following part of its course, we took the flagstone path, used by walkers on the Pennine Way, past the church and out into fields at the edge of the town. We paused at the cemetery to pay our respects at the memorial cross for the victims of the Lunds railway crash of Christmas Eve 1910. Nearby are many unmarked paupers graves, people whose passage through life had left them without the resources to mark their resting place. The pathway led towards the nearby village of Gayle, but we didn't have time to go that far. In the distance, though, we could see an 18th century mill building on the banks of Gayle Beck, and beyond that, the pale outline of Wether Fell.

We came in a full circle back into the western end of Hawes where the retail market was in full swing. Most of the stalls were set up in the wide main street, but some were in the fuggy warmth of the Market Hall which dates from 1898. Time was getting on. We had arranged to catch the bus back outside the Market Hall, but we had twenty minutes to spare so we nipped across the road for a glass of 'Old Peculier' in "The Crown Hotel". Bang on time Raymond appeared in his mini-bus to whisk us back to Garsdale. At £1.20 each way, the fare seemed ludicrously cheap, and being the only passengers we felt rather guilty at being provided with what amounted to a personal taxi service at bus fare prices. Raymond allayed our fears: "Don't worry, you're being sponsored by the county council; thank them, not me!"

Information

BUSES – *Throughout the summer the minibus meets several trains at Garsdale on a daily basis, telephone 0228 812812 or 0969 50682 for details. On summer Sundays the service is extended to Askrigg and Swaledale for the benefit of ramblers. In winter the bus only operates between Garsdale and Hawes on Tuesdays and Saturdays and prospective passengers must book their journey no later than 8pm the previous day on 0969 50682.*

FACILITIES – *Hawes is the main centre for Upper Wensleydale. It is particularly well endowed with inns, most of which provide meals and accommodation, and cafes. Shopping facilites are good but not extensive, there are branches of the Midland and Barclays banks. Craftshops and antique shops are well represented and there is a small antiquarian bookshop with a good range on local topography.*

TOURIST INFORMATION – *Station Yard, Hawes. Tel: Hawes (0969) 667450. Closed during the winter.*

UPPER DALES FOLK MUSEUM – *Station Yard, Hawes. Tel: Hawes 667494. Open late March – October daily. Small admission charge.*

Market Day, Hawes.

TUCKED under the hem of Little Fell, the line descends at the ruling gradient of 1 in 100 with a brief easing at the site of Mallerstang sidings. From the western windows of the train the view is restricted to outcrops of moss covered rock, waterfalls and the occasional precipitous pasture wrought tenaciously out of the fellside. From the eastern side of the train the view is splendidly reminiscent of that offered by the best Alpine railways. The Eden, encouraged by the support of numerous becks and gills, pursues a northbound course along the valley floor. Lonely whitewashed farmhouses stand sequestered at the end of steep, rutted tracks. The world does not beat a path to such doors. Post vans, mobile grocers, and animal feed reps are possibly the only regular visitors to farmyards where a marked degree of rural poverty exists beyond the ken of Whitehall's statisticians. On the opposite bank of the Eden the escarpment rises steeply to the rocky outcrops of Mallerstang Edge, beyond which lies Swaledale.

The only community of any sort is the hamlet of Outhgill whose chapel can be seen beside the river. It has associations with Lady Anne Clifford, an indomitable 17th century gentlewoman still venerated in the Dales and the Eden Valley. She was born at Skipton Castle in 1590 into a family of aristocrats who later moved to London where she was brought up on the peripheries of the Royal court. In 1605 her wealthy father died but she was disinherited by his brother and nephew. She spent the next thirty years campaigning to regain her inheritance but it was not until the death of her cousin that her father's estate reverted to her. In the interim the family's estates in the north of England had been allowed to fall into rack and ruin and Lady Anne set about reviving them. To reach Outhgill she travelled along the old green road which follows the escarpment of Abbotside Common. In her diary for 1663 she wrote of going "over Cotter in my coach – where I think never a coach went before – and over Hellgill Bridge into Westmorland". She went on to restore Pendragon, Brough and Appleby castles and was buried in St Lawrence's church, Appleby in 1676.

A widening of the trackbed level with Outhgill marks the site of Mallerstang sidings. The Midland Railway had an aversion for 'facing points' on main lines. And so instead of providing loops which a train could enter at one end and leave at the other, they preferred to let their goods trains reverse into a siding, when the need arose for them to be overtaken by an express or when entering a goods yard. As built, the only facing point between Settle and the outskirts of Carlisle was at Appleby where a branch from the down main line linked up with the North Eastern Railway. In the 'up' direction there were no facing points at all until loops were laid at Blea Moor during the second world war to speed traffic up. Mallerstang sidings were taken out of use in 1969.

To the east the ruins of Pendragon Castle can be seen. Legend has it, rather fancifully, that this was once the home of King Arthur's father, Uther Pendragon. It makes a nice story, but logic suggests that the building is more likely to have originated as a tower of defence against Scottish attacks in the 12th century. Lady Anne Clifford spent the Christmas of 1663 here and wrote of watching the moon over Wild Boar Fell and listening to the Eden gurgling over its bed. Pendragon is perhaps the most romantically ruined of several fortified buildings in the vicinity. Little remains of Lammerside Castle a couple of miles to the north on the west bank of the Eden, whilst either side of Kirkby Stephen there are fortified houses at Wharton and Smardale.

Views of Pendragon are swallowed up by the deep cutting which forms the approach to Birkett Tunnel. The telegraph wires are carried over the tunnel, making their slightly surreal way across the top of the moor. These wires, and their associated posts, are one of the less obvious traditional aspects of the railway landscape which survive on the Settle & Carlisle, along with a dwindling number of semaphore signals and sections of track which still make the wheels go clickety-clack; the sort of things which elsewhere have disappeared almost without being noticed. Whilst you are inside the tunnel nature effects a quick scene change and, on emerging from the northern portal, you sense that the mountainous country which has become familiar since Horton-in-Ribblesdale, is being left behind. From the eastern side of the train you can enjoy a last lingering view of the youthful Eden picking its way around the foot of Birkett Common under the receding headlands of High Pike Hill, Tailbridge Hill, and Nine Standards Rigg; the last with its nine cairns clearly countable if visibility is good. Next time you see the river it will have widened considerably. To the west a green road runs briefly beside the line and then the brakes go on for Kirkby Stephen.

Kirkby Stephen 'West' as it was once known, emphasises that the Midland's priority was to reach Scotland, and that the serving of any communities encountered on the way was of secondary consideration. The station is nearly two miles out of town and a hundred and fifty feet higher. Had the line been built any lower for the benefit of Kirkby Stephen, the southbound climb to Ais Gill would have been much steeper. In any case, Kirkby Stephen was already connected to the North Eastern Railway's Darlington, Barnard Castle and Tebay line which had opened independently in 1861, serving a station much closer to the centre of the town. It also bears remembering that in the days before the motor car, people were accustomed to walking much further. Nowadays we baulk at having to leave the car at the far end of the supermarket car park, in Victorian times country folk thought nothing of walking several miles to shop, or work, or be schooled at the nearest market town.

The Midland station at Kirkby Stephen was built to the same specification as Settle and Appleby. A large goods shed was provided and a cattle dock capable of handling up to ten wagons at a time. Goods trains stopped serving the yard in 1964 and it has inevitably become the premises of a bulk liquids road haulier. Part of the station building, built of a creamy coloured stone, is still used by British Rail's engineering department. The original shelter on the 'down' platform has been replaced by what looks like an off the shelf garden shed. Chickens scratch in the mud in the adjacent field and occasionally find their way on to the platform. The busy main road from Kendal to Brough passes beneath the line and is lined on one side by former railway workers bungalows and cottages. The signal box, a replacement structure of 1950s vintage, remains in use for the time being, and if the train looks like being late, you can telephone the signalman and ask him why.

The mountains might be behind you now, but the line's tallest viaduct is just around the corner. With the rounded towers of Smardale Hall in view to the east, the railway crosses Smardale Viaduct, a gracefully curving structure built from grey limestone. Beneath it runs the delightfully named Scandal Beck which has trickled down from Ravenstonedale to find the Eden. A ford carries the parallel country road from Waitby to Crosby Garrett across the beck. To the west you get a sudden and all too brief glimpse of what appears to be a mirror image of the viaduct. It's no optical illusion, but rather the *other* Smardale Viaduct, a noble fourteen arch structure which carried the North Eastern line over the hills and along the valley of the Lune to Tebay. This route, closed in 1962, passed beneath the southernmost arch of the Midland viaduct.

A short tunnel and another viaduct preceed the site of Crosby Garrett station. From the viaduct the village looks beguiling. A beck runs between a jumble of houses separated by little parcels of green, and the church stands proudly on an artificial mound thought to be the site of an Iron Age temple. The locals prefer the story that the devil made the mound so as to deter the old and infirm from seeking the solace of their maker. Crosby Garrett station was built in a cutting and you can see the indentations left by the long demolished waiting rooms.

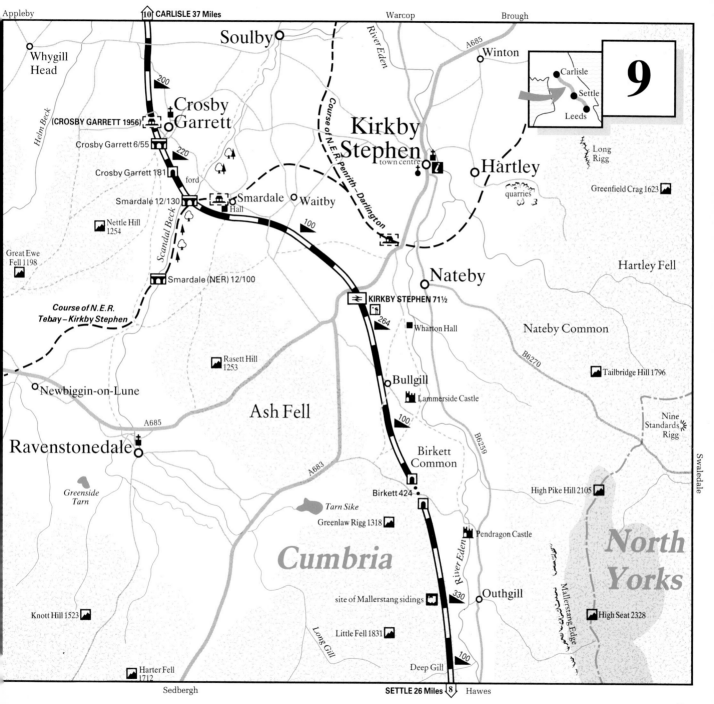

Appleby

10 CARLISLE 37 Miles

Soulby

Warcop

Brough

River Eden

A685

Winton

Whygill
Head

200

Long
Rigg

9

Carlisle

Settle

Leeds

Helm Beck

Crosby
Garrett

(CROSBY GARRETT 1956)

Crosby Garrett 6/55

220

Crosby Garrett 181

ford

Smardale 12/130

Smardale
Hall

Waitby

Kirkby
Stephen

town centre

Hàrtley

quarries

Greenfield Crag 1623

Course of N.E.R. Penrith–Darlington

Scandal Beck

Nettle Hill
1254

100

Great Ewe
Fell 1198

Smardale (NER) 12/100

*Course of N.E.R.
Tebay – Kirkby Stephen*

Nateby

Hartley Fell

Newbiggin-on-Lune

A685

Rasett Hill
1253

Ash Fell

KIRKBY STEPHEN 71½

264

Wharton Hall

Nateby Common

B6270

Tailbridge Hill 1796

Bullgill

100

Lammerside Castle

Ravenstonedale

Greenside
Tarn

Tarn Sike

A683

Greenlaw Rigg 1318

Birkett
Common

Birkett 424

B6259

Nine
Standards
Rigg

Knott Hill 1523

Cumbria

River Eden

Pendragon Castle

High Pike Hill 2105

*North
Yorks*

Mallerstang Edge

site of Mallerstang sidings

330

Outhgill

High Seat 2328

Long Gill

Little Fell 1831

Harter Fell
1712

Deep Gill

100

Sedbergh

SETTLE 26 Miles **8**

Hawes

Swaledale

43

EVERY journey has its less eventful passages, and this is the Settle & Carlisle at its most anodyne. North of Crosby Garrett the countryside is pleasantly unspectacular. On a less dramatic railway ride this innocently rolling countryside might be regarded as a welcome interlude between urban sprawl. On the Settle & Carlisle it gives you an excuse to see if you can operate the Sprinter's push-button toilet doors without embarrassment. Five times out of six you'll probably catch someone with their pants down because the travelling public haven't yet come to terms with the function of the lock button.

It is difficult to accept that Griseburn Viaduct marks the half-way point between Settle and Carlisle. Subconsciously one imagines the middle to be somewhere up in the mountains. But, in reality, the route climbs abruptly from Settle to Ais Gill, before falling more gently towards Carlisle. Ian Nairn, the late architectural and travel writer, referred to the section north of Ais Gill as the line's "long diminuendo" and that sums it up very well. Griseburn Viaduct carries the railway over Helm Beck, a tributary of the Eden. North of the viaduct the Midland Railway had a ballast quarry, the remains of which can be seen on the western side of the line.

Helm Tunnel preceeds Great Ormside and another abandoned station, closed in 1952. One registers the blurred shapes of the now familar Derby Gothic buildings. Rarely can a railway have exhibited such homogenity in its accoutrements. Most main lines were built piecemeal by independent companies at the outset of the Railway Age. Travel from Euston to Glasgow and you pass over the tracks of several constituents. Similarly, from Kings Cross to Edinburgh. Even the Great Western's line from London to the West Country displays a remarkable diversity in architectural styles. Only on the now closed Great Central Railway from Marylebone to the East Midlands and South Yorkshire was such a prevaling pattern of building styles so obvious.

North of Great Ormside the line crosses the Eden for the first of two times. As we anticipated, the river has grown in stature since last seen back at Birkett Common. After passing under the line it curves gracefully towards Appleby around the base of a wooded hill, accompanied by a pleasant riparian footpath. To the east the high fells return, stretching up towards the Lune Forest, a sponge-like wilderness of watershed country known only to walkers on the Pennine Way and soldiers out on target practise.

"a sponge-like wilderness of watershed country known only to walkers on the Pennine Way and soldiers out on target practise".

From the western side of the train, the turreted Norman tower of Appleby Castle comes into view. It looks a bit like one of those simple model forts you might have played with as a child; far removed, at any rate, from scenes of violence and aggression. But, by all accounts, it stood like a red rag to the bull-like tendencies of the Scots, who repeatedly sacked the town throughout the Middle Ages, the worst occasion being in 1388, from which, some say, Appleby has never really recovered!

As the train slows down for the Appleby stop it passes a large dairy on the east side of the tracks. There is no rail connection now – British Rail abandoned the carriage of milk throughout the system in the early Eighties – but once a daily special of milk tankers was despatched from here to Cricklewood, so that Londoners could savour the creamy taste of milk produced by the Eden Valley's contented cows.

Appleby's long platforms were built for Anglo-Scottish expresses and Sprinters look lost in them. Only the occasional charter train does them justice now; the days of the "Thames-Clyde Express" (which only deigned to call at Appleby towards the end of its exalted existence) and "The Waverley" are long past. The Settle & Carlisle is like a proud football club with a tradition of first division status now languishing in the third. FOSCL have lobbied British Rail to revive the St Pancras – Leeds – Glasgow itinerary with a 125 unit, but the response so far has been lukewarm. What this club needs is a star signing!

The waiting room at Appleby is warm in winter. A stove glows and waiting passengers share the comfort of strangers. Behind the ticket counter leading railman Bob Palmley, or his relief, Vanda Braid, goes about the routine of running a railway station. In a perfect world all small town stations would be like this. Instead they are more normally staffless, devoid of facilities and vandalised beyond redemption.

"In a perfect world all small town stations would be like this."

With time on your hands you can take in the nuances. A gorgeous lattice-work footbridge, picked out in red and cream, links the two platforms. At the southern end of the 'up' platform the local Rotary Club have rebuilt the former water tank so that steam specials can be refreshed here once again. On the side of the station building a plaque commemorates Eric Treacy, a bishop and one of the great railway photographers, who collapsed and died on Appleby station whilst photographing a steam special. He was of the view that the Settle & Carlisle, York Minster and Hadrian's Wall constituted the three chief man-made wonders of northern England; he apparently forgot to list the fourth, Farrah's Original Harrogate Toffee.

Have you noticed that the station buildings here are built of brick, not stone? British Rail's proposals for refurbishing the station include provision of a new toilet block with disabled facilities and the leasing of part of the offices for retail use. Ceramic flooring will be installed in the waiting hall along with new wall coverings and softer lighting. The original Midland timber seating will be retained and refurbished. In 1991 Appleby became the northern terminus of the "Cumbrian Mountain Express". Extra layover time here allows for lost time to be regained without delay to the southbound departure and offers passengers more time to stretch their legs than was the case when the steam hauled excursion continued to Carlisle. On most days when excursion trains are using the Settle & Carlisle, 'The Friends' operate a bookstall on the station.

When charter trains stop-over at Appleby, they take refuge in the former link line between the Midland and North Eastern railways. This track saw more regular use until 1989 when freight traffic to and from the Army depot at Warcop was withdrawn, largely because of the closure threat hanging over the main line. Warcop is six miles south-east of Appleby and this section of the North Eastern's Eden Valley line was retained after the rest was lifted in 1962, following withdrawal of the Penrith – Kirkby Stephen – Darlington trains. Despite the loss of the Army traffic the rails remain intact and British Rail have offered the line to any interested group for potential use as a preserved steam line. Meanwhile those with an enthusiasm for such things can stroll over to the old North Eastern station and sigh over the remains: a level crossing, goods shed and station house, and a rusty track leading into who knows what of a future.

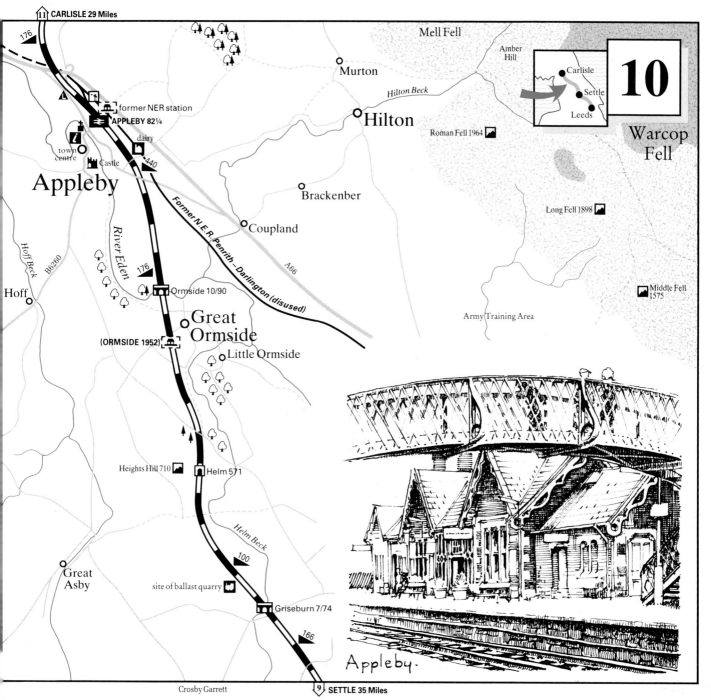

11 CARLISLE 29 Miles

176

Murton

Mell Fell

Amber Hill

Hilton Beck

Hilton

Roman Fell 1964

10

Carlisle

Settle

Leeds

Warcop Fell

former NER station

APPLEBY 82¼

dairy

town centre

Appleby

Castle

440

Brackenber

Long Fell 1898

Coupland

River Eden

176

A66

Former N.E.R. (Penrith – Darlington (disused)

Hoff Beck

B6260

Hoff

Ormside 10/90

Great Ormside

(ORMSIDE 1952)

Little Ormside

Middle Fell 1575

Army Training Area

Heights Hill 710

Helm 571

Helm Beck

Great Asby

100

site of ballast quarry

Griseburn 7/74

166

Crosby Garrett

Appleby.

9 SETTLE 35 Miles

45

CROSS FELL, the highest point in the Pennines, steals the show as the northbound train skips downhill through the aptly named Eden Valley. The railway has dropped out of the higher hills – the former station at Newbiggin is 400 feet above sea level – but on the eastern side of the train, the Pennine chain continues to fill the horizon. The broad summit of Cross Fell is said to bear some snow at least for three-quarters of the calendar. Legend has it that St Augustine named it, after building a cross on its summit to ward off evil spirits. But any ghost prepared to haunt its heathery tops must be a hardy soul indeed. Ask anyone who has toiled to its top whilst tackling the Pennine Way, or huddled behind the stone-built shelter on its summit, taking refuge from the Helm Wind; a violent north-easterly prevalent in late winter and early spring. Mike Cudahy, the fell runner and first man to complete the 270 miles of the Pennine Way in under three days, wrote of the mountain being "magnificent, but not trustworthy," and "not beautiful, but commanding of respect." The River Tees rises on Cross Fell's sinewy south-western shoulder before striding through Yorkshire and Cleveland to disgorge itself into the North Sea. Yet just a few clumps of bog grass away, lies the source of Crowdundle Beck, which elects to flow westwards down past the screes of Wildboar Scar and, passing under the railway near Newbiggin, to join the Eden at Temple Sowerby.

"The broad summit of Cross Fell is said to bear some snow at least for three-quarters of the calendar."

If Cross Fell is unquestionably the star of this part of the Pennines, it has a strong supporting cast. To the south lies Great Dun Fell, unmistakeably topped by the Civil Aviation Authority's radar station, whilst drawn about the skirt of the fells stand a sequence of conical summits, known locally after the Lakeland fashion, as pikes. Morton Pike, Dufton Pike and Knock Pike can be picked out easily from the train as long as the weather is at all kind. To West Riding eyes they have the look of spoil tips, albeit lofty ones, a misleading impression apt to be reinforced by the location of gypsum mining in the area. This is an activity which has flourished in the vicinity for two centuries. The current works at Kirkby Thore, operated British Gypsum, is engaged in the manufacture of plasterboard. The gypsum is extracted from three local drift mines and a surface quarry. A conveyor belt links the various sites with the main works, and this can be seen passing beneath the railway north of Long Marton. Once the rock has reached the works it is crushed, ground, heated and added to chemicals to produce raw plaster. A glimpse from the passing train of overgrown sidings and a solitary semaphore signal indicates that the works was once connected to the railway. Indeed it had its own shunting locomotive and, throughout the 1950s, over a hundred thousand tons of gypsum was being despatched from here by rail each year. Now, inevitably, the works' products are despatched by British Gypsum's own fleet of juggernauts which can be seen parked in rows beside the railway where the sidings once were. Mining subsidence forces trains to slow when passing Kirkby Thore and a system of infra-red lights measure any movement in the trackbed which might cause derailments.

A melancholy trio of abandoned stations – Long Marton, New Biggin and Culgaith – punctuate the line's progress. All three closed in 1970, the villages they served being hardly large enough to sustain a bus service, let alone individual railway facilities. Indeed, in the case of Culgaith, the Midland Railway had no intention of providing a station at all until they had their corporate arm twisted by the local vicar. One imagines their engineer unbending to the cleric's demands over a glass or two of good port. In the event Culgaith station opened four years after the rest of the line, the most peculiar thing about it being its architectural style, quite unlike the standardised buildings along the rest of the line. Built from local stone, the single storey structure, with its steeply pitched roof, looks more like the lodge house to a country seat. Nowadays it, and the adjacent crossing-keeper's house, are private homes, though the signal box remains in use, guarding the nearby level crossing.

"One imagines their engineer unbending to the cleric's demands over a glass or two of good port."

At New Biggin (spelt as two words by the Midland Railway, but as one by the Ordnance Survey) the station building, station-master's house and a quartet of employees cottages remain intact and in use as private dwellings. The station building here was of the smallest S&C type, and built from a fresh creamy-coloured stone, with sandstone trimmings. To the north of the station, a viaduct carries the line over Crowdundle Beck, formerly the boundary between the old counties of Westmorland and Cumberland. From the eastern side of the train there is a tantalising glimpse of the National Trust property of Acorn Bank whose aromatic herb garden is open to the public. Long Marton station housed a community centre, but looks rather the worse for wear nowadays. The goods shed has suffered the ultimate indignity of becoming a lorry park, a fate dealt out to a number of these handsome, gothic-windowed buildings. In its heyday the shed at Long Marton provided cover for up to three wagons whilst they were being loaded or unloaded, and temporary storage for outgoing and incoming commodities, originating from, or destined for the local parish. In this ubiquitous era of the lorry, we tend to forget the significance of the local railway goods yard, a pivotal undertaking in the economy of the village and its rural hinterland. Couched almost in the shadow of Dufton Pike, an attractive group of Midland Railway cottages stand below the northern end of Long Marton viaduct.

Envious stares may be emanating from those seated on the western side of the train, as they crane their necks to pick out the salient features of the Pennine backbone, but they have their own mountain range – if a more distant one – to enjoy, not to mention the gorgeous Eden itself, living easily up to its name, as it comes back into view beyond the two short tunnels at Culgaith. The Lakeland summits are too distant, and the train too swift, to be anything more than a tantalising blur, but the river weaves a captivating spell which more than compensates; after all, you can sit on the opposite side on the way back! Between Culgaith and Langwathby the River Eamont makes an entrance, its confluence with the Eden occuring amidst broad meadows which provide a fertile wintering ground for wild geese. The Eamont has its origins in the Lake District, flowing out of Ullswater, and down past Penrith, where it is joined by the Lowther, which runs off the northern flank of Shap Fell. The canoeist, William Bliss, wrote endearingly of the Eamont and Eden in his book, "Rapid Rivers", published in 1935. He describes a whitsuntide night when he camped beside the confluence having come down from Kirkby Stephen in his Canadian canoe. The next morning, at dawn, he swam in the two rivers, attempting, but being thwarted, to make heady against the current in the Eamont. Then, as the sun peeped over the shadowy outline of Cross Fell, he had fried a freshly caught trout over a camp fire and breakfasted as simply as satisfyingly as a man might have done on the same spot a thousand years before him.

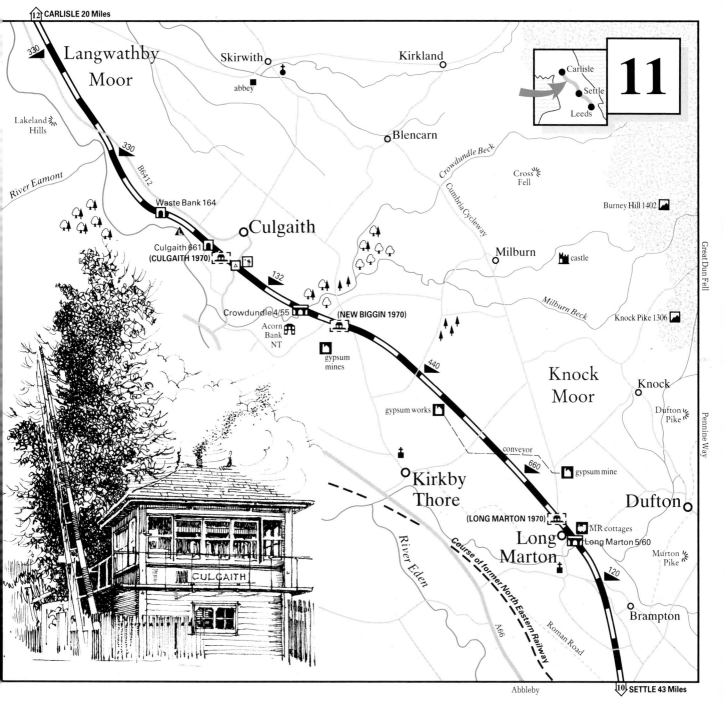

330

Langwathby
Moor

Skirwith

Kirkland

abbey

330

B6412

Lakeland
Hills

River Eamont

Blencarn

Crowdundle Beck

Cumbria Cycleway

Cross
Fell

Burney Hill 1402

Waste Bank 164

Culgaith

Milburn

castle

Culgaith 661
(CULGAITH 1970)

132

Milburn Beck

Knock Pike 1306

Crowdundle 4/55

(NEW BIGGIN 1970)

Acorn
Bank
NT

440

gypsum
mines

Knock
Moor

Knock

Dufton
Pike

gypsum works

conveyor

660

gypsum mine

Dufton

Kirkby
Thore

MR cottages

Long Marton 5/60

(LONG MARTON 1970)

Long
Marton

Murton
Pike

River Eden

Course of former North Eastern Railway

120

Brampton

A66

Roman Road

Abbleby

CULGAITH

Great Dun Fell

Pennine Way

11

Carlisle

Settle

Leeds

IN THE HEYDAY of the Midland Railway there was a nightly departure from London St Pancras on the stroke of midnight, a 'Scotch Corridor Express' conveying sleeping car passengers for Glasgow St Enoch. The train reversed at Leeds, acquired a fresh pair of engines and made its way over the Settle & Carlisle as dawn broke – in the summer months at any rate – over the Pennine *massif*. Perhaps many an early riser, inquisitively drawing their compartment blinds as the train snaked its way down the Eden Valley, was fooled into thinking that they had already crossed the border, for the scenery hereabouts evokes an uncanny sense of Scotland; especially so to the north of Lazonby, as the line winds through the pinewoods of the Eden Gorge. In the vicinity of Baron Wood, the railway tunnels beneath a brackeny expanse of moorland, grazed – as if to complete the illusion – by herds of Highland cattle. This is hunting, shooting and fishing country personified. On the 'Glorious Twelfth' of 1911 the Midland ran no less than fifteen special trains of sportsmen intent on bagging more than their fair share of grouse. A lengthsman once caught sight of a salmon poacher standing 'up to his teeth' in the River Eden to escape detection. On one of the January days we researched this section of the line, the local hunt was out in force, their scarlet jackets and grey steeds in tuneful harmony with the colours of the Inter City charter train also on the line that day.

Sleeping car expresses gradually evaporated from the timetables of the Settle & Carlisle line after the Beeching years, when the Anglo-Scottish overnight traffic was concentrated on the West Coast Main Line. Ironically though, in almost clandestine fashion, three Saturday night and Sunday morning sleeping trains were still using the S&C as a diversionary route during 1991. The undoubted romance of the sleeping car, however, has no place here. It is the landscapes of the Settle & Carlisle that draw your attention now, so let's get back to daylight hours and consider the line's character as it see-saws with gradients which, generally, descend towards Carlisle, but face occasional climbs, such as those south of Lazonby and Baron Wood, to facilitate progress around the rocky sandstone bluffs and outcrops of the Eden Gorge.

The railway crosses the river for only the second time by way of Eden Lacy viaduct; four of the bridge's six piers being permanently washed by the northward flow of the Eden's waters, an indication of the growing breadth of the river since it was previously crossed by the line at Ormside, south of Appleby. Downstream of the viaduct the river foams across a weir at the site of a former mill. In medieval times there was a pack-horse bridge here as well. Immediately south of the viaduct lies the site of the once extensive Long Meg mineral sidings. A pair of rusty loops remain intact, presided over by a 'locked-out' signal box. Silver birch and rosebay willow-herb, those eager colonisers of wastegrounds, flourish where lines of trucks once waited to be loaded with anhydrite, a source of sulphur shipped in considerable tonnages to an ICI chemical works at Widnes, near Liverpool. In fact, this commodity was more

or less the last significant freight traffic to originate from the Settle & Carlisle, being withdrawn when the works closed in 1973.

The wayside stations of Langwathby and Lazonby re-opened in 1986 following a grant being made available by the local authority. In the intervening sixteen years since closure the goods sheds at each station had found new uses: the shed at Langwathby having been annexed by a poultry products firm rejoicing in the name of Frank Bird, whilst that at Lazonby has become part of a bakery. Lazonby goods yard did a sterling trade in livestock carriage because of the close proximity of an auction mart. In the years following the First World War something like 2,500 wagons of livestock were being dealt with per annum. Both station buildings were built of Eden Valley sandstone to an identical design. Standing now on their unstaffed platforms, it is difficult to shake off a sense of sadness. One misses the company of a loquacious porter, the soliloquy of the waiting room fire in winter, the rattle of milk churns being deposited for despatch by the next train. But if there is an inescapable regret that stations such as these are no longer the focal point of the villages they serve, one can only be grateful that they function at all. Local FOSCL members see to it that timetable and tourist leaflets are usually available and that the gardens are neatly tended, whilst, in common with the other unstaffed stations on the line, the public can use a telephone link with the nearest signalman, to ascertain the whereabouts of any late running trains. In any case, waiting for trains offers the welcome opportunity for self-communion. At Langwathby this can be shared with the rooks cawing from their adjacent tree-top nests, whilst at Lazonby you have the company of the souls resident in the churchyard which overlooks the 'up' platform.

South of Lazonby Tunnel stood a set of sidings serving a railway owned sand pit. The sand extracted from here was conveyed to various motive power depots for use as an aid to the adhesion of locomotives on greasy rails or steep gradients. One imagines a fair amount of the stuff was used on the Settle & Carlisle route itself. Another isolated set of sidings can still be seen at Baron Wood. Here forestry was the *raison d'etre*, a local sawmill cut the timber into pit props which were taken out by rail to various collieries up and down the country. The scene from the carriage window between Lazonby and Armathwaite really is ravishing; ample compensation for the loss of mountain scenery. Seen in glimpses between the tunnels and the cuttings, the Eden cascades down its rocky bed framed by tumbling woodlands of birch and pine. On the east bank of the river at the point where the Croglin Water joins the river, are the famous Nunnery Walks, a series of pathways stretching down through divine woodlands past a dramatic waterfall and gorge. Hidden from view on the railway side of the Eden, close to the railway cottages at Baron Wood, is Sampson's Chamber, a cave used as a hiding place by a navvy who had murdered one of his colleagues during the building of the railway. Eventually he was captured and later hanged at Carlisle

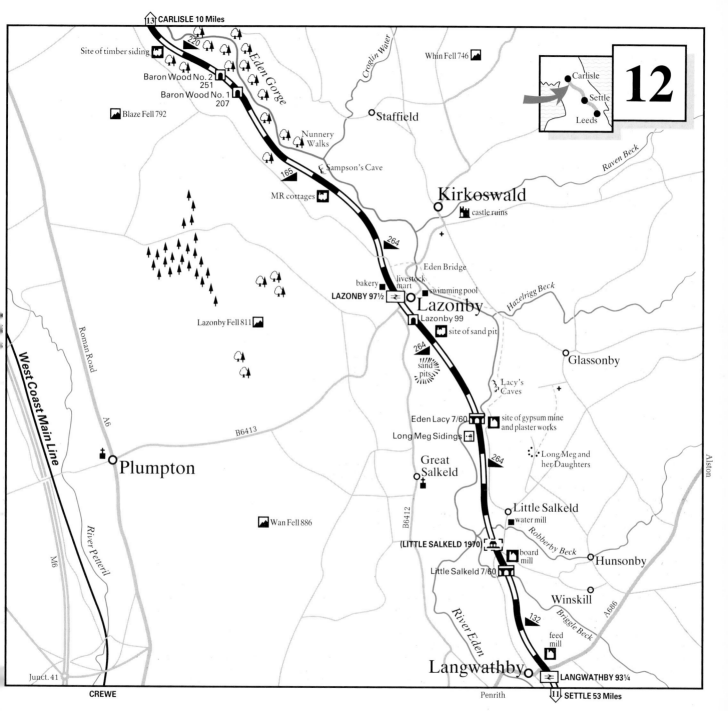

13 CARLISLE 10 Miles

Site of timber siding

Baron Wood No. 2
251
Baron Wood No. 1
207

Blaze Fell 792

Eden Gorge

220

Croglin Water

Whin Fell 746

Carlisle
Settle
Leeds

12

Nunnery Walks

Staffield

Raven Beck

Sampson's Cave

165

Kirkoswald

MR cottages

castle ruins

264

Eden Bridge

bakery   livestock
          mart

Hazelrigg Beck

swimming pool

LAZONBY 97½

Lazonby

Lazonby 99

Lazonby Fell 811

site of sand pit

Glassonby

264

sand
pits

Lacy's
Caves

Long Meg and
her Daughters

West Coast Main Line

Roman Road

A6

B6413

Eden Lacy 7/60

site of gypsum mine
and plaster works

Long Meg Sidings

Plumpton

Great
Salkeld

264

Little Salkeld

River Petteril

Wan Fell 886

B6412

water mill

(LITTLE SALKELD 1970)

Robberby Beck

Hunsonby

board
mill

Little Salkeld 7/60

Winskill

M6

Junct. 41

River Eden

132

Briggle Beck

A686

feed
mill

Langwathby

LANGWATHBY 93¼

CREWE

Penrith

11 SETTLE 53 Miles

Alston

49

Walkabout No. 4 – Temptations of Eden

It was one of those incandescent days which March has on credit terms from May. No deposit, easy payments, no hats, no coats required. In the garden of the station house at Lazonby the local FOSCL rep looked up from his weeding and wished us a pleasant walk. His father had been the stationmaster here in the days when there had been forty wage packets to issue every Friday: porters, signalmen, platelayers, and the men who worked the quarry sidings down at Long Meg. "It was one of the busiest stations on the line," he recalled wistfully, "the goodsyard was full of wool, rabbits, eggs and coal." Nowadays the goodsyard is full of bakery vans and the platelayers' cottages are holiday homes. But the realities of the late-twentieth century economy couldn't detract from such an auspicious morning, and the churchyard was full of daffodils as we turned left along the by-road signposted 'Baron Wood'. The livestock market was deserted. We had missed the Wednesday auction by a day. In the autumn lamb sales, the man at the station had told us, they deal with anything up to 30,000 sheep a day at Lazonby.

Half a mile along the road we turned right into a field at a public footpath sign pointing to 'Eden Bridge'. A beck, gurgling down to meet the Eden, made the going squelchy underfoot. We skirted a flock of ewes yet to lamb, and reached the handsome 18th century sandstone bridge. On the far bank we turned right on to another field path signposted 'Dale Raven'. The path followed the river for about a mile. We were surprised by a pair of oystercatchers taking to flight from the riverbank. Reaching a wood which hides Hazelrigg Beck's confluence with the Eden, we took briefly to the road, then, crossing the nearby bridge, turned into the wood, up a path signposted 'Lacey Caves' and 'Little Salkeld'. Emerging from the trees, we crossed a style and went into a field at some height above the river. Gradually the path descended to the riverside and then passed through a conifer plantation.

Little Salkeld

Wooden planks spanned rivulets trickling towards the river and the wood was full of birdsong.

Suddenly, the path lurched steeply upwards and twisted over a rocky promontory. As it came down again a side path issued from it towards the river. This led to Lacy's Caves, a series of chambers hewn out of the soft sandstone, said to have been the work of Colonel Samuel Lacy who lived at Salkeld Hall in the 18th century. One story suggests that the colonel employed a man to live in the caves as a hermit, adding an aura of romantic dissolution to the neighbourhood. Even in the sunshine the caves seemed spooky. We gingerly proceeded from one to the next, half expecting to come upon something unpleasant, and having nerved ourselves to explore each cave in turn, we were glad to regain the daylight and return to the main path. Gladder still, we were to see the railway crossing the river just upstream – the civilising influence of the steel rail. The path we were following was used by miners from Kirkoswald on their way to and from work at the Long Meg mine. Remnants of the machinery, the detritus of industrial endeavour, protruded from the undergrowth. Down below us the Eden foamed poetically over a weir, or 'force' as they say hereabouts. Upriver a fisherman had waded out into the current to cast his lure. A 'Sprinter' swooshed by across the viaduct.

We went on our way, passing cattle munching hay where once there had been sidings. A sharp zig-zag took us past a sub-station, beyond which we joined a metalled road parallel to the railway. A yellowhammer flew out of the hedgerow ahead of us and we looked down upon the empty signal cabin which had once controlled shunting at the mine. On the far side of the line the Eden wound gorgeously past fields being put to the plough, seagulls following in the tractor's wake. Little Salkeld slept in a noonday silence. These days there is not enough life here to support a shop or a pub, but down where the Robberby

Water passes under the road to Langwathby, a watermill goes about its unobtrusive business, a throwback to a simpler age. It isn't operated as a tourist attraction; it works long hours for its living. Visitors may call in to buy flour, muesli or porridge oats, but no elaborate interpretive packages are laid on for them. Simply, if the miller isn't otherwise engaged, he will show you round his empire with a quiet pride. Ducking under low rafters, we peered into shadowy corners to acquaint ourselves with the ancient machinery. Then we were led round the back to see where the millrace fed the overshot wheel. We were gratified to learn that business was brisk, with a large export order for Norway on the books. A telling reflection on modern farming though, was the information that the grain they were using at Salkeld had come all the way from Worcestershire, to meet with the owner's insistence that it should be organically grown.

With a kilo of porridge as a souvenir, we left Little Salkeld and headed up the road to Long Meg stone circle. On our right the Pennine chain stood recumbent in the middle distance. The sun was warm on our backs as we approached the stones. Long Meg and her Daughters are no Stonehenge, but neither do they suffer from the Wiltshire circle's popularity. We had them to ourselves, but didn't attempt to count them. Legend has it that if anyone came up with the same number twice, the witch and her daughters would come to life, and we were taking no risks!

The path away from the circle led through a waymarked gate at the top right hand corner of the field. Further gates and waymarkers brought us through a field of sheep to the curiously isolated church of St Michael's, Addingham. Apparently the village of the same name stood on the banks of the Eden and was washed away by a particularly nasty flood in the 13th century. We walked through the churchyard, rejoined the road, and presently came to Glassonby, another village now bereft of pubs and shops. From the village green we took the road signposted 'Kirkoswald'. As Glassonby was left behind the road dipped and we were confronted with a panoramic view of the river flowing through a magical patchwork of pasture and woodland towards the Eden Bridge. A curlew flew over our heads making for the moors to our right. The road was largely traffic free and we made rapid progress in the direction of Kirkoswald, crossing once again, the stone bridge over Hazelrigg Beck.

Half an hour later we were sitting on a bench outside the pub with the sun glinting on our pale amber tumblers of 'Old Peculier'. The first building we had seen on entering Kirkoswald had had the year 1622 carved on its red sandstone lintel. Further perambulation had revealed some

modern interlopers from the 18th century. We had watched rooks soaring about the ruined 15th century towers of the old castle, and passed the strange bell tower of St Oswald's, built separately from the church which stands at the foot of a hill whilst the belfry sits on the top. The steep main street lay dormant in the afternoon warmth like a Mediterranean village on siesta. There was little incentive to move. Lazonby was only twenty minutes walk away and there was almost an hour until the train was due. What could we do but order another round?

Information

DISTANCE & CONDITIONS
Start and end at Lazonby station. OS Landranger sheets 86, 90 & 91. Nine miles, allow 3½ hours net walking time.

REFRESHMENTS
Refer to the Gazetteer for details of pubs and shops in Lazonby. Kirkoswald has three pubs and a general store.

PLACES TO VISIT
The Watermill – Little Salkeld. Millshop open Mondays to Fridays 9.30am to 12.20pm and 2pm to 5.30pm. Tel: Langwathby (076881) 523.

Long Meg and her daughters.

EMERGING from the brief darkness of Armathwaite Tunnel, the line continues to descend before levelling-out to cross a curving viaduct, then climbs again to reach Armathwaite station, another which re-opened in 1986. It is one of the most picturesque locations on the whole of the Settle & Carlisle. Conifers overshadow the platforms and the sandstone station buildings, the latter somewhat marred by an unsympathetic extension. Far below, the chimney pots and rooftops of the village are glimpsed in its riparian setting. The dominant building is Armathwaite Castle, which had its origins as a 'pele' tower designed to ward off Scots marauders. The present structure is largely 18th century and is now occupied more peaceably.

The station is used as the local British Legion clubhouse; the goods shed by a fertilizer firm. Beyond the station precincts, beside the by-road which climbs over the forested shoulder of Hill Rigg, stand the former stationmaster's house and a typical terrace of Midland Railway staff cottages. The disused signalbox remains to the north of the station beside the 'up' line, and 'The Friends' intend to refurbish it as an attractive piece of railway architecture. A waiting room, on the same side, provides prospective southbound passengers with a modicum of shelter.

Noticeably higher above the Eden now, than back at Langwathby and Lazonby, the line progresses northwards over two more lofty viaducts, encountering in the process a rare level crossing, and passing the 300 mile marker from St Pancras. Three further closed down stations are met on the last lap into Carlisle. The station building at Cotehill has been demolished but the stationmaster's house and staff cottages remain. A short branchline led from here to a plaster works at Knothill, but this was dismantled during the second world war. Between Cotehill and Cumwhinton stations a number of sidings were provided to serve a variety of industries, notably a brick and tile works and a plaster and gypsum works; the latter was still being shunted by a steam tank engine in the early Seventies. Howe's Siding signalbox, which controlled these lines, is still in use, governing activities on the main line. Once there were thirty-five signal boxes between Settle and Carlisle. In 1991 only seven were still in daily use.

"Once there were thirty-five signal boxes between Settle and Carlisle. In 1991 only seven were still in daily use."

Cumwhinton station remains in a good state of repair, despite having been closed in 1956. Much of it is used by a timber company now. On December 29th, 1904 a gang of platelayers came upon the carcass of a 'full grown grey male wolf' which had been decapitated by a passing train. Despite local rumours to the contrary, this was not evidence of the survival of such creatures in the wild, but rather the unsavoury fate of an animal which had escaped from a private zoo. The Midland Railway's most northerly station was at Scotby, but it closed as early as 1942, the village also being served by a station on the Carlisle–Newcastle line.

As the Settle & Carlisle approaches the border city, the River Eden – so influential in the line's course and character since Kirkby Stephen, twists away on its roundabout course towards the Solway Firth. By rail it is six miles from Cotehill to Carlisle – by river, fourteen. The fells also recede from view as the train slows past acres of wasteground formerly occupied by Midland Railway goods sidings and locomotive facilities. The official extremity of the Settle &

Carlisle was at Petteril Bridge Junction where the line from Leeds met the North Eastern Railway's route from Hexham and Newcastle. Midland trains were granted 'running powers' over North Eastern tracks into Carlisle station. Interestingly, Bradshaw quoted the distances from Euston and St Pancras to Carlisle as 299 and 308 miles respectively; without referring closely to the map one would have thought that the Midland route's wanderings through the East Midlands and West Riding would have resulted in a significantly wider margin. The London & North Western route, though, was much the easier, and there was no reversal involved, as the Midland had to contend with at Leeds. In the Edwardian era, The LNWR could offer a schedule half an hour faster than the Midland's between London and Carlisle, but the Midland wooed its travelling public with superior rolling stock and delectable scenery.

Railways converge on Carlisle like electricity pylons on a power station. Historically, the reasons for this were not so much commercial – Carlisle was never much of an industrial centre – as geographical. From north and south the lines were squeezed towards Carlisle by the inhibiting presence of Solway Firth and the border hills. The boundary between England and Scotland added to the complexity of lines for, even 250 years after the Act of Union, the developing railways considered the territories of the former enemies sacrosanct. As a result, no less than seven railway companies built and operated lines to Carlisle, and, remarkably, in spite of the Beeching years and other subsequent rationalisations and closures, six of these routes remain in use today. Before the 'grouping' of the railways in 1923, a walk along Carlisle's platforms would present a technicolour dreamcoat of locomotive and rolling stock liveries. Royal blue engines from the Caledonian Railway, black from the London & North Western, red from the Midland, yellowy-brown from the North British, and three distinctive shades of green from the North Eastern, Glasgow & South Western and Maryport & Carlisle companies. The rolling stock added further colour to the kaleidoscope, most notably the gorgeous red-brown and white carriages of the Caledonian. Happily, following years of slavish adherence to their dreary corporate blue, British Rail are enthusiastically consorting with colour again. A lot of people think it would be nice if the Settle & Carlisle trains were given the added identity of their own colour scheme, crimson lake – a throwback to Midland colours being the most popular suggestion – but the Sprinters currently used on the line also work on other parts of the railway system where their distinctive Settle & Carlisle livery would look out of place.

Drifting past rusty sidings, and a retail park built on the site of Cowans Sheldon, a firm once famous throughout the world for the construction of railway turntables and breakdown cranes, the train from Leeds clatters over pointwork and under the electric catenary of the West Coast main line, before coming to a rest in the imposing atmosphere of Carlisle's 'Citadel' station. It is everything that Leeds City is not. It has character and strength and exudes a sense of history, so that it is easy to imagine its platforms still filled by the great expresses of the past. High stone walls, the colour of the succulent flesh of Solway sea trout, support soaring, pigeon haunted girders fenestrated by myriad panes of glass. It is a steam age cathedral colonised by the thrumming traction of the era of high technology. A surprising surfeit of railway staff perform mysterious rites and rituals. When the Settle & Carlisle Sprinter comes to a halt in platform 6, boys with soapy buckets rush forward to clean its windows. Rattling trains of parcel trolleys weave intricate patterns between knots of waiting passengers. Out along the platform ends, impervious to the elements, trainspotters gaze at passive rows of locomotives. In quiet gothic corners travel book writers scribble purple prose on the back of pocket timetables . . .

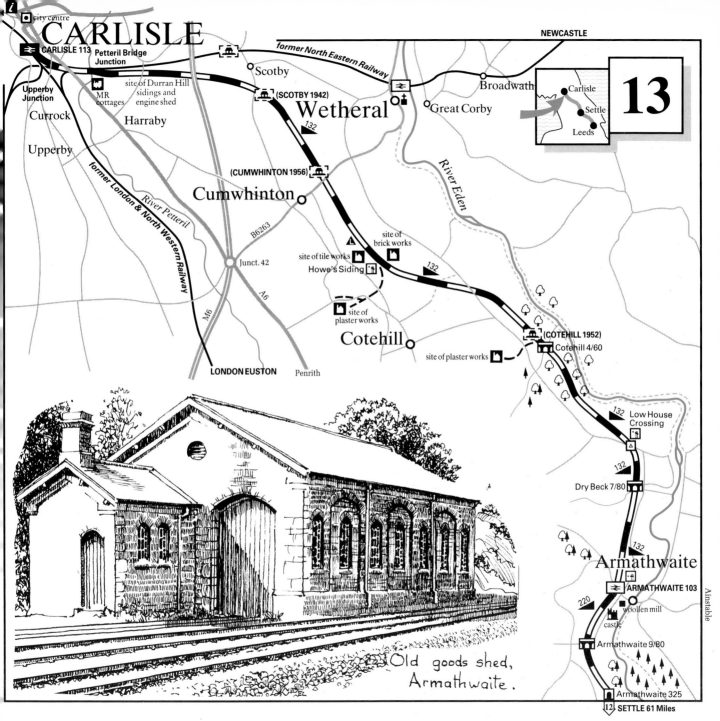

CARLISLE

- city centre
- **CARLISLE 113** Petteril Bridge Junction
- Upperby Junction
- Currock
- Upperby
- Harraby
- MR cottages
- site of Durran Hill sidings and engine shed

former London & North Western Railway

River Petteril

Junct. 42

M6 A6

LONDON EUSTON Penrith

B6263

Scotby

(SCOTBY 1942)

Wetheral

132

(CUMWHINTON 1956)

Cumwhinton

former North Eastern Railway

NEWCASTLE

Broadwath

Great Corby

River Eden

site of tile works

Howe's Siding

site of plaster works

132

Cotehill

site of brick works

site of plaster works

(COTEHILL 1952) Cotehill 4/60

132 Low House Crossing

132 Dry Beck 7/80

132

Armathwaite

220 **ARMATHWAITE 103**

woollen mill

castle

Armathwaite 9/80

Armathwaite 325

12 SETTLE 61 Miles

Ainstable

13

Carlisle
Settle
Leeds

Old goods shed, Armathwaite.

Using this Guide

Thirteen one inch to a mile maps portray the route of Leeds, Settle & Carlisle railway. These are accompanied by a running commentary on the course of the line. Emphasis is given to the northward journey, but the details are equally relevant for travel in the opposite direction. Maps and text appear on facing pages for easy reference.

The commentary concentrates on describing the course of the railway and on discussing points of associated interest. For further details of the places served by the line, turn to the gazetteer. This, along with a brief portrait of the character of each city, town or village, includes details of recommended places of refreshment and (where appropriate) accommodation, shopping facilities and visitor centres. Please note however that facilities of this sort are susceptible to change and the advice of the local Tourist Information Centre should be sought where essential accuracy is required. Additionally the gazetteer lists brief details of suggested walking routes from each station along the line. Reference to the relevant Ordnance Survey "Landranger" map will flesh out more detail and suggest further itineraries to suit personal choice.

Interspersed with the main text and maps are a series of 'Excursion' and 'Walkabout' mini-features. These are presented in the 'first person' for the sake of atmosphere, and are designed to make readers aware of the many possibilities for exploration and enjoyment which exist within the framework of the Leeds, Settle & Carlisle corridor.

When to Go

A journey on the Leeds, Settle & Carlisle can be rewarding at any time of the year. It is a line, as the old cliche goes, for all seasons. Each change in the calendar is reflected through the broad windows of the train, and the views which you thought you knew well in summer take on a quite different aspect when snow covers the fells or when mist shrouds the moors. At the beginning and end of the year the trains are less busy and you have correspondingly more comfort and space in which to assimilate the drama of the landscapes which the railway passes through.

Plan ahead and avoid the crowds. Received wisdom suggests that the heaviest demand for travel is northwards out of Leeds mid-morning, returning from Carlisle around teatime. Try and make sure you travel in the opposite direction to this prevailing pattern if you possibly can. Moreover, it is not widely known that return tickets from the Carlisle end of the line are cheaper than those from Leeds. The Settle & Carlisle should not be about crowds. Its attraction lies in its ability to present its travellers with an impression of wilderness which they can retain to inspire them through the routine of urban life.

The publishers are grateful to the following individuals and companies who have contributed to the compilation and production of this guidebook: Brian Sutcliffe and Pete Shaw of FOSCL; Paul Snowden, Geoff Bounds and Paul Holden of BR; Apollo Canal Carriers, British Gypsum, Crossley & Evans, GKN Kirkstall, Leeds Reference Library, and Tilcon.

The illustrations are from the 'express' pen of Eric Leslie. The maps were produced from OS 6″ base material 1909–38 updated by personal survey.

Personal thanks from 'MP' to: Eric Leslie, Malcolm Barnes, Mark Curnock, Graham Pitman, Terry Wright, Alan Brittan, Brian Collings, Ken and Mike at Cordee and Mr & Mrs Goss. Adrenalin from 'The Deaks' ("all to do and only hours . . ."), optimism from 'JMP', and tolerance from 'JAP' otherwise engaged on a much more important project of her own.

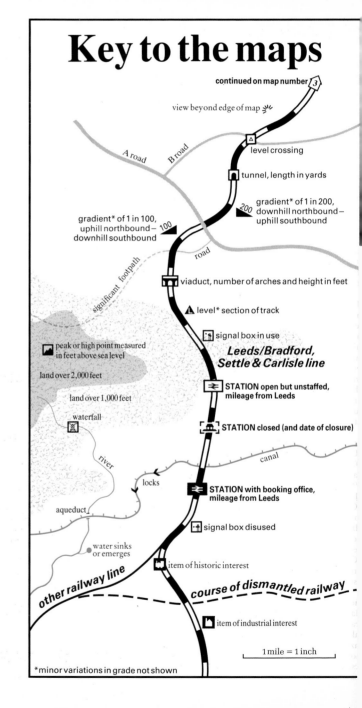

Key to the maps

continued on map number 3

view beyond edge of map

A road   B road

level crossing

tunnel, length in yards

gradient* of 1 in 200, downhill northbound – uphill southbound

gradient* of 1 in 100, uphill northbound – downhill southbound

significant footpath

road

viaduct, number of arches and height in feet

level* section of track

signal box in use

Leeds/Bradford, Settle & Carlisle line

peak or high point measured in feet above sea level

land over 2,000 feet

land over 1,000 feet

waterfall

STATION open but unstaffed, mileage from Leeds

STATION closed (and date of closure)

canal

river

locks

STATION with booking office, mileage from Leeds

aqueduct

signal box disused

water sinks or emerges

item of historic interest

other railway line

course of dismantled railway

item of industrial interest

1 mile = 1 inch

*minor variations in grade not shown

GAZETTEER

A

Appleby

ntil 1974 the county borough of Westmorland, Appleby [w]one of the most interesting and historic small towns in [no]rthern England, and there is no better way to arrive [he]re than by train along the Settle & Carlisle line. The [ce]ntre of town is across the River Eden, a pleasant 5 [mi]nute walk downhill from the station. The main [th]oroughfare, Boroughgate, sweeps imposingly down [fro]m the castle to the market square. Bordered by lawns [an]d lime trees, it exudes an unostentacious dignity. At [eit]her end stand obelisks topped by sundials, known as [th]e High Cross and Low Cross respectively, they mark [th]e boundaries of the market. At the upper end of [B]oroughgate an archway leads to a courtyard of al[m]shouses built for the widows of the town by Lady Anne [Cl]ifford in 1651 and serving the same function to this [da]y. The main building at the foot of Boroughgate is the [16]th century Moot Hall. Beyond it a row of cloisters [at]tractively screen the approach to the parish church of [St] Lawrence.

Appleby lets its hair down once a year for the famous [Ho]rse Fair which takes place on the second Wednesday [in] June. Gypsies and traders, travelling people and tourists [de]scend on the town for up to a week before the fair, [m]any of them camping out on Fair Hill to the east of the [ra]ilway station. Traditional vados, or horse-drawn vans, [are] the camping ground with luxury trailers. Stalls are [se]t up and fortunes are told. Camp fires are lit in the [ev]ening over which can be heard the lilt of Romany music. [Th]e business of buying and selling horses is taken particu[la]rly seriously and the animals are taken down to the [Ed]en for a wash, an altogether picturesque sight in an [al]together picturesque town.

Refreshments & Accommodation
[TU]FTON ARMS HOTEL – Boroughgate. Tel: Appleby [0]7683) 51593. Well appointed town centre hotel. Re[sta]urant and bar meals.
[W]HITE HART HOTEL – Boroughgate. Tel: Appleby [51]598. Les Routiers recommended two star hotel.
[R]OYAL OAK INN – Bongate. Tel: Appleby 51463. [Fo]rmer coaching inn on the railway side of the river.
[MI]DLAND HOTEL – adjacent station. Marston's, bar [m]eals. Snug 'local' ideal for a quick drink or snack bet[w]een trains. B&B Tel: Appleby 51524.
[C]OPPER KETTLE – Boroughgate. Breakfasts, coffees, [lu]nches & teas. Comfortable cafe.
[Fi]sh & chip shop on 'The Sands', 2 minutes from station.

Shopping
[M]arket day on Fridays, early closing on Thursdays. [Br]anches of Barclays and Midland banks. Some good [ba]kers shops like 'Appleby Bread Shop' and 'Bells of [La]zonby'. VG late shop open daily until 10pm. Interesting [sh]ops include EAST OF EDEN, crafts and herbal cosme[tic]s, and the COURTYARD GALLERY, specialists in [pa]intings, pottery, jewellry and glass.

Places to Visit
TOURIST INFORMATION CENTRE – Moot Hall, Boroughgate. Tel: Appleby (07683) 51177.
APPLEBY CASTLE – Boroughgate. Open daily Easter to end September. Admission charge. Tel: Appleby 51402. 11th century Norman keep and Rare Breeds Survival Trust.

Local Transport
BUSES – Services to Kendal and Penrith. Tel: Carlisle (0228) 812812.

Walking
An East Cumbria Countryside Project leaflet describing a circular walk of 8 miles including Appleby and Great Ormside is available from the Tourist Information Centre. Three miles to the north-east of Appleby station is the picturesque village of Dufton, a watering place on the 'Pennine Way'. A 7 mile circular walk around Dufton Pike is described in another ECCP leaflet.

Armathwaite

On a warm summer's day there is no finer Settle & Carlisle destination than Armathwaite. Don't go and swelter with the crowds at Carlisle. Step off the train here and treat yourself to lunch at one or other of the comfortable inns, then spend the rest of your time lazing by the riverbank watching the fat fish rise for flies. The suffix 'thwaite' points to the Old Norse origins of this peaceful village. For many years salmon netting was important to the local economy. An 18th century sandstone bridge spans the river at the site of an earlier ford. The tiny sandstone church has a stained glass window designed by Burne-Jones.

Refreshments & Accommodation
DUKES HEAD HOTEL – Front Street. Bar & restaurant meals, teas and coffees, accommodation. Tel: Armathwaite (06992) 226.
FOX & PHEASANT HOTEL – far side of bridge. Meals and accommodation. Tel: Armathwaite 400.

Shopping
Post office and general store.

Places to Visit
Eden Valley Woollen Mill – village centre, opposite post office. Designer weaving. Small shop open daily Easter to mid October. Tel: Armathwaite 457.

Walking
The East Cumbria Countryside Project publish a leaflet describing a 6 mile circular walk based on Ainstable on the east bank of the Eden. An unclassed road runs southwards from Armathwaite through Baron Wood Park to Lazonby and makes for an enjoyable walk.

B

Bingley

When you walk out of the station and reach the main street, Bingley seems too overcome by traffic to hold much appeal for the visitor. But away from the A650 and the dominant office block of the Bradford & Bingley Building Society, there are several enclaves of calm worthy of exploration. One interesting feature is the Butter Cross and Market Hall thought to date from 1212 when King John gave the town its first market charter. The cross used to stand in the main street but was moved in 1888 to make way for the traffic.

Refreshments
BROWN COW – pleasant, wood-panelled Timothy Taylor pub adjacent to Ireland Bridge, does good lunches. Accommodation. Tel: Bradford (0274) 569482.

Shopping
Market on Wednesdays and Fridays. Early closing on Tuesdays. Safeway supermarket but not a great deal of other shopping to be had. Damart have a factory shop on Park Road (Tel: (0274) 568211).

Walking
Via Cross Gates and the Druid's Altar to Thwaites Brow and Keighley (4 miles), or by way of the canal past 'Five Rise Locks' to Micklethwaite and across the top of Ilkley Moor to Ilkley (6 miles) from where you can catch the train back to Shipley etc.

Bradford

Compared with Leeds, Bradford is like the dark side of the moon. But Bradford has its pride and a gritty Yorkshire arrogance which enables it to cock a snook at its sleek and upwardly mobile neighbour. Everywhere are the architectural echoes of its Victorian and Edwardian heyday when it was a textile centre of world renown. Buildings like the City Hall, the Wool Exchange and the Alhambra Theatre reflect a past prosperity based on the manufacture of worsted cloth. Massive mills and warehouses surround the city centre. One particular area was known as 'Little Germany' in reference to the large number of merchants of that nationality who made their home here in the 19th century. A hundred years later another influx of imigrants created an Asian community which brought fresh impetus to Bradford's character. Bradford is not directly served by Leeds – Carlisle trains, but there are frequent connections to the city from Shipley, and its the sort of place which, sooner or later, you should take the trouble to visit.

Refreshments & Accommodation
VICTORIA HOTEL – Bridge Street (adjacent 'Interchange' station). Comfortable middle-range hotel with bar and restaurant facilities. Tel: Bradford (0274) 728706.
TRIBELLS – Sunbridge Road (city centre). A Bradford institution: huge fish & chip restaurant where they serve 'a pot of tea and bread & butter' with every meal.
NEW BEEHIVE INN – Westgate. Camra recommended Edwardian pub still with lighting by gas. Bar food, family room and wide range of mostly Yorkshire brewed real ales.
FLAVOUR OF ASIA – not a restaurant, but a leaflet available from the Tourist Information Centre describing

many of the numerous ethnic restaurants and food stores for which Bradford is justly famous.

Shopping

Shopping facilities in Bradford are generally less ambitious than those in Leeds, but the Kirkgate precinct houses many well known chain stores, whilst the Rawson and John Street market halls are bustling centres of local produce and retailing. A leaflet available from the Tourist Information Centre lists the many mill shops where you can find a textile bargain by cutting out the middle man.

Things to Do

NATIONAL MUSEUM OF PHOTOGRAPHY, FILM & TELEVISION – Princes View. Open Tue-Sun. Tel: Bradford (0274) 727488. Bradford's premier attraction.
TREADWELL'S ART MILL – Upper Park Gate. Open daily. Tel: Bradford 306065. Gallery of modern art & sculpture in restored wool warehouse in 'Little Germany'.
COLOUR MUSEUM – Grattan Road. Open Tue-Fri afternoons and Sats. Tel: Bradford 390955. Unusual museum devoted to the development of colour in our lives.
INDUSTRIAL MUSEUM – Moorside Road. Open Tue-Sun. Tel: Bradford 631756. Museum of Bradford's textile past housed in former spinning mill. Buses 614 or 634 from Market Street.
TOURIST INFORMATION CENTRE – City Hall. Tel: Bradford (0274) 753678.

C
Carlisle

Following his television journey up the Settle & Carlisle in 1972, Ian Nairn found Carlisle to have "no sense of identity", a lack of character reflected visually by the "cacophony and mess" of the market place. Someone in the town planning office obviously took his well meant criticisms to heart, for nowadays Carlisle has retrieved its dignity and become an attractive place to visit. The round towers of the Citadel which face the station entrance set the tone, beyond them the visitor can follow English Street to the Market Square, pedestrianised since Nairn's day. Here the old town hall has been refurbished as a visitor centre, a point of departure for closer exploration of "The Great Border City".

Refreshments & Accommodation

CUMBRIA HOTEL – Court Square. Right outside the railway station this Ashley Courtenay and AA recommended hotel provides comfortable accommodation and is a handy venue for bar or restaurant meals. Tel: Carlisle (0228) 31951.
CUMBRIAN KITCHEN – station forecourt. Coffee shop open throughout the day serving snacks and meals.
ROYAL HOTEL – Lowther Street. Family run budget priced hotel just 3-4 minutes walk from the station. Tel: Carlisle 22103.
HOWARD ARMS – Lowther Street. Opposite entrance to Lanes Shopping Centre, Camra recommended pub offering Theakstons and bar lunches. Nice tiled frontage and atmospheric interior.

Shopping

The city is excellent for shopping and in The Lanes shopping centre they have managed to create a modern precinct of considerable character. To our way of thinking, however, pride of place should go to the delightful covered market, a Victorian retailing centre rivaling Citadel station in its architectural splendour. It houses a fine array of stalls, many specialising in Cumbrian delicacies.

Things to Do

TULLIE HOUSE – Castle Street. Open daily. Much vaunted celebration of Carlisle and The Borders turbid history, including section on the city's railway heyday. Tel: Carlisle (0228) 34781.
CASTLE – Castle Way. Open daily. Well preserved fortification dating from the 11th century. Tel: Carlisle 31777.
CATHEDRAL – Castle Street. 12th century church built from red sandstone, one of the country's lesser known ecclesiastical treasures.
TOURIST INFORMATION CENTRE – Old Town Hall. Tel: Carlisle (0228) 512444.

Cononley

A more modest version of Silsden dominated by two former mills; one long used by a manufacturer of electrical motors, the other housing a car showroom and an ice cream factory. Just as at Silsden, a beck runs engagingly, arm in arm, with the main street. Here, though, the effect is much gentler and residential.

Refreshments

Two cosy pubs: THE RAILWAY (John Smiths) and NEW INN (Taylors). Fish & chips too.

Shopping

Post office and newsagent, food store, and butcher.

Walking

Wonderful walks, east or west. You can cross Cononley Moor into Lothersdale to join the Pennine Way. Follow that famous footpath north to Gargrave to rejoin the railway; a memorable 12 miles! Alternatively, cross the Aire, and climb past Farnhill Hall up to the Jubilee cairns on Bradley Moor. The view from the summit is breathtaking, a marvellous prospect of middle Airedale. Return via Farnhill (a delightful village) and the Leeds & Liverpool Canal to Silsden and the railway.

Crossflatts

A suburb of Bingley. The station is handy for Bingley's famous 'Five Rise Locks' and for Micklethwaite Studio Workshops, a group of craft workshops housed in a former textile mill at the edge of Rombalds Moor. Telephone Bradford (0274) 561209 for further details.

D
Dent

A northern Clovelly, but with the character of mint cake rather than the cloying nature of cream fudge, Dent huddles under the shoulders of the fells, its houses cuddled together to protect themselves from the elements. Cobbl streets wind past ancient, whitewashed buildings a somehow, despite its popularity with tourists, the vill retains a sense of reality, of a community going about daily business. Business now is farming and tourism, b a couple of centuries ago Dent was a centre for the maki of gloves and stockings. The inhabitants were then kno as the 'terrible knitters of Dent': not a reflection on th apptitude, but terrible in the sense of a great capacity work. The trade relied on packhorse trains for the carria in to the town of wool and worsted and the export of the finished goods. But the development of mechanised woollen industry in the West Riding, bet connected by canal and then railway to the rest of country, doomed the town to a spiral of decline.
Bear in mind that the village is 5 miles from the stati A lot of people enjoy the walk down and make arran ments to take the local taxi back – see below.

Refreshments & Accommodation

THE SUN INN – Main Street. A classic country p comfortably furnished and quiet (no piped music, jukebox) with photographs of various Dales landma adorning the walls. Home-cooked bar meals, home b wed beer and bed & breakfast. One of the best reas for coming to Dent. Tel: Dent (05875) 208.
STONE CLOSE CAFE – Main Street. Mike Harding c this 'the best little cafe in the Dales' and it is also fe in the "Good Food Guide". Only open at the weeke in winter. Also do b&b. Tel: Dent 231.
GEORGE & DRAGON HOTEL – Main Street. Bar restaurant meals. Accommodation. Also serves 'Dent ter'. Tel: Dent 256.

Shopping

Post office and general stores; gallery, wool shop a craft shop.

Things to Do

DENT CRAFTS CENTRE – located approx 2 miles w of Dent on Sedbergh road. Demonstrations by lc craftsmen. Coffee shop and restaurant. Tel: Dent 40(
HIGH HALL FARM – Dent. Conducted tours of farm and its rare breeds in the afternoons daily (ex all year round. Tel: Dent 331.

Local Transport

TAXIS – Tel: Dent (05875) 432 (or 202/3). Single from station to village or vice versa around £5. Can up to 6 people. Book well ahead to avoid being strande

Walking

See 'Walkabout 3'. Dent itself can be reached on from the station via Cowgill and the 'Dales Way' (5 m with the option of returning to Ribblehead station southbound trains only) across the back of Whernsic

F
Frizinghall

Suburban station on the Bradford line, handy CARTWRIGHT HALL art gallery and LISTER PAR

G

Gargrave

e River Aire waters the village green, flowing seduc-
ely beneath a three-arch bridge past stone cottages built
apparent random to the main street. Aylesburys and
allards keep up a cacophony of duck talk which goes
me way at least to drowning the roar of traffic on the
55. That Gargrave is a stopping off point for the Dales
d the Pennine Way is made apparent by the prolifera-
n of shops and cafes catering for this passing trade.

freshments & Accommodation
NCHOR INN – on A65 at west end of village. Smart
rewers Fayre' pub/restaurant offering accommodation.
rge adventure playground for children. Tel: Skipton
756) 749666.
ALESMAN CAFE – high starch meals for hungry cyc-
s and walkers.
MONDSONS – fish & chip cafe closed Monday but
en Sundays.

opping
od selection of shops catering for most needs. Barclays
nk open briefly on Mons & Weds. Several antique
ps. Early closing on Tuesdays.

us Connections
nnine Motors have their garage here and their attractive
ange buses supplement public transport along the Skip-
n – Settle corridor. Tel: Skipton (0756) 749215.

alking
e 'Walkabout 1'. For an alternative consider the Pennine
ay up to Malham served by bus from Gargrave and
ipton.

Garsdale

scattered community with no real centre. The railway
tion is actually located at Garsdale Head where there
e lines of former railway staff cottages, a number of
lated farmhouses, a Mount Zion chapel and an inn.

freshments & Accommodation
IE MOORCOCK INN – approximately a mile from
station at the junction of the Sedbergh-Hawes and
kby Stephen roads. Theakston's ales, bar meals and
d & breakfast. Tel: (0969 667) 488.
ST MUDBECKS – 5 minutes walk from station. Bed
breakfast. Tel: (05396) 21328.

s Connections
'Excursion 4' for details of Hawes link. During the
mmer there is also a bus link with Sedbergh. Tel: Carlisle
28) 812812.

alking
Grisedale and Uldale – both off the beaten track – or
Hawes via Tarn Hill, Cotterdale and the Pennine Way.

H

Hellifield

The village seems to have experienced a decline commen-
surate with its railway status. The livestock market has
closed and the village shops and inn seem little more than
a blip on the consciousness of the A65's hurrying
motorists. But for the archaeologist of railway history
Hellifield is a pilgrimage not to be eschewed. Go now,
before the ghosts are exorcised by development or demoli-
tion. Stand in awe under those great expanses of iron
and glass canopies with the Midland initials and dragon
like wyverns, mourn the trackless bays now strangled by
vegetation, let your footsteps echo down the sinuous, tiled
subway and stroll down Station Road past the railway
workers terraces remembering that at the turn of the century almost two-thirds of Hellifield families were occupied
in railway work. *Sic Transit Gloria Mundi*

Refreshments & Accommodation
THE BLACK HORSE – village centre. Food and accom-
modation. Tel: Hellifield (07295) 223.
Fish & chip shop nearby.

Shopping
Newsagent, village stores, post office, butcher and
Barclays Bank (limited hours Mon & Tue only) in village
centre. Corner store at end of station drive.

Walking
Potentially nice ramble, station to station, to Gargrave
mostly on tracks and paths via Hellifield Moor, Airton,
Bell Busk and Coniston Cold: 10 miles.

Horton

Horton-in-Ribblesdale is base camp for the 'Three Peaks',
and a stopping off point on the Pennine Way and the
more recently devised Ribble Way, and at most times of
the year it hooches with folk in cagoules wilting under
the weight of enormous haversacks. Yet, apart from the
picturesque narrow bridges which span the Ribble and
Brants Gill, and the ancient, largely Norman church of
St Oswald's, the village itself is not that intrinsically attractive, a good proportion of the local economy being derived
from quarrying and lorry driving. The Rural Development
Commission have also built a group of small industrial
units to attract other local industries to the neighbourhood.

Refreshments & Accommodation
PEN-Y-GHENT CAFE – a mecca for walkers, cavers,
cyclists and visitors generally who value the enthusiasm
and local knowledge of the staff. They know, too, how
to cater for hungry appetites born of the fells and also
stock an excellent range of Dales literature and outdoor
equipment. Tourist Information as well. Open daily ex
Tue. Tel: (07296) 333.
CROWN HOTEL – food & accommodation. Tel: Horton 209.
GOLDEN LION HOTEL – food & accommodation. Tel:
Horton 206.
Additionally there are many guest houses in the village

offering a wide range of facilities, contact the cafe (see
above) for up to date details.

Shopping
Post office stores and small gallery. See also Pen-Y-Ghent
Cafe.

Walking
See 'Walkabout 2' for the ascent of Penyghent. There are
too many alternatives to list adequately here. The most
obvious one is the ascent of Ingleborough via Sulber (4
miles each way), but why not try the Ribble Way, northwards to Ribblehead (7 miles) or southwards to Settle (8
miles).

K

Keighley

An immediately likeable town with few airs and graces,
Keighley's prosperity was built on textiles and engineering, though one of the main employers now is Peter Black,
suppliers of clothing and other goods to Marks & Spencer.
Architecturally, stone predominates and there are many
dignified buildings in the main thoroughfares, especially
the Edwardian public library in North Street.

Refreshments
Keighley is the home of Timothy Taylor's prize-winning
ales and many of the pubs in the town serve these excellent
beers. Pizza houses are also thick on the ground, whilst
there seem to be more fish & chip shops than you'd expect
to find in Morecambe or Bridlington.

Shopping
For a town of its size Keighley is a surprisingly good
shopping centre, and Cavendish Street, the first street of
shops you reach from the station, has an unusual canopy
overhanging its pavement on one side. The Airedale Shopping Centre houses most of the better known retail chains,
there's a market hall, and several factory shops such as
Peter Blacks.

Things to Do
EAST RIDDLESDEN HALL – 1 mile north-east of railway station (bus connections). Open Easter – October
but not daily: telephone Keighley (0535) 607075 to check.
17th century manor house and tithe barn owned by the
National Trust. Tea room and NT shop.

Walking
WORTH WAY – a 5½ mile linear or 11 mile circular
waymarked series of paths linking Keighley with
Oxenhope and Haworth. Leaflets available locally or
from the Tourist Information Centre in Haworth. Tel:
(0535) 42329.

Kirkby Stephen

"A place for licking wounds and replenishing stores"
wrote Wainwright in the guidebook to his own "Coast
to Coast" walk. Settle & Carlisle travellers will tend to
see it from a different point of view, and are likely to be
put off by the thought of the long walk along a busy road

without a pavement for part of the way. But the occasional bus meets the train and there are taxis to be hired and, to our way of thinking, Kirkby Stephen is as interesting to explore as Appleby. The town is blessed with a good proportion of handsome buildings in a wide variety of architectural styles and periods. We particularly liked the Temperance Hall with its slightly 'primitive' figure of the Goddess of Temperance dressed in blue above the doorway, and the old butter market standing very fetchingly in front of the imposing parish church, known as the 'cathedral of the dale'. Many of the buildings are built from the local brockram stone, an unusual mixture of limestone and sandstone which takes on a rosy hue when the sun shines. Away from the bustle of the main street there are quiet walks to be had beside the River Eden, which can be crossed by a pack horse bridge.

Refreshments & Accommodation
PENNINE HOTEL – Market Street. Accommodation, bar meals. Tel:
KINGS ARMS – Market Street. Accommodation, bar meals. Tel: KS (07683) 71378.
WHITE LION – Market Street. Marston's, bar meals.
COBBLESTONES – cosy tea rooms in the High Street.
COAST TO COAST – fish & chip shop on North Road named after Wainwright's walk. Two others nearer the town centre.

Shopping
The town is the recognised shopping centre for a wide district. Monday is Market Day and has been since 1361, the stalls stand in an attractive setting overlooked by St Stephens. There are several craft and antique shops, a gallery and a bookshop. Thursday is early closing and there are branches of Barclays and Midland banks. A Spar grocery is open daily until 10pm.

Walking
Nine Standards Rigg is a strenuous but rewarding climb to the east by way of Hartley (10 miles there and back).

Things to Do
TOURIST INFORMATION – Market Square. Tel: KS (07683) 71199.

Local Transport
BUSES – services to/from Brough, Barnard Castle, Tebay etc. Tel: Cumbrian Connections on Carlisle (0228) 812812. Some buses connect the station with the town centre. Make enquiries!
TAXIS – Tel: KS (07683) 71682, 71741. Single fare to town centre averages £2. Book ahead!

L

Langwathby
17th century houses built from the dark red local sandstone overlook the medieval village green, which is just a stone's throw from the station. The local children still dance round the Maypole on the green each third Saturday in May. The bridge carrying the Alston – Penrith

road across the River Eden was swept away by floods in 1968 and the 'temporary' replacement is still there. The local farming economy is boosted by an animal feeds mill.

Refreshments
THE SHEPHERDS INN – village centre. Whitbread beers and bar meals. Tel: Langwathby 335.

Shopping
Post office stores by village green.

Things to Do
ACORN BANK – National Trust gardens located 5 miles south-east of Langwathby and partially visible from the railway. Open daily April to October.

Bus Connections
Bus links with Keswick, Penrith and Alston (for the South Tynedale Railway). Tel: Carlisle (0228) 812812.

Walking
An East Cumbria Countryside Project leaflet describes a 3½ mile circular walk starting from Langwathby and taking in Edenhall. Copies of the leaflet usually available at the post office stores or from the TIC in Appleby.

Lazonby
Famous for its Autumn sheep sales, Lazonby is an otherwise quiet village pleasantly situated beside the River Eden. It has close connections with Kirkoswald to which it is linked by a fine 18th century river bridge. Lazonby's most significant building is the Victorian church, which stands on a mound overlooking the station.

Refreshments
MIDLAND HOTEL – a Matthew Brown pub adjacent to the station. Food usually available.
JOINER'S ARMS – 3 minutes east of station. Whitbread, bar meals.

Shopping
Co-Op stores and post office/bakery (nice fresh cakes).

Things to Do
NUNNERY WALKS – privately owned woodland walks beside the Eden Gorge and Croglin Beck. Small admission charge payable at adjacent guest house and tearooms. Located 3 miles north of Lazonby via Kirkoswald. Tel: Lazonby (076883) 537.

Walking
See 'Walkabout 4'.

Leeds
Yorkshire seems to specialise in one syllable cities: York, Hull, Leeds; bluff, blunt names which go with the county's gruff image. York is the tourist honeypot, Hull the enigmatic port, but it is Leeds which has its feet most firmly placed in the present; Britain's third largest city, the commercial capital of the region, and a centre for sport, culture and retailing. If you have preconceived notions of Leeds holding no appeal for visitors, cast your eye down the following list of attractions and think again!

Refreshments & Accommodation
QUEENS HOTEL – City Square. Former railway hotel of startling 1930s Art Deco design. Now owned by Trust House Forte and located beside the station. Tel: Leeds (0532) 431323.
WHITELOCKS – Turks Head Yard, Briggate. Magnificent Edwardian city pub offering bar and resturant food Youngers beers.
ADELPHI – by Leeds Bridge. Another Edwardian masterpiece. Lunches on weekdays. Tetley beers.
THE GRANARY CAFE – Granary Wharf (beneath the station, access via Neville St). Wholefood and vegetarian cafe just a few minutes walk from the station.

Shopping
The Headrow and Briggate are historically the city's main shopping thoroughfares. These are supplemented by several modern precincts. Markets are held daily in the super Edwardian surroundings of the City Market. A trio of elegant Victorian arcades can be found close to junction of The Headrow and Briggate. Granary Wharf is a development of craft shops in the 'Dark Arches' beneath the station. The elliptically shaped Corn Exchange – another of Cuthbert Broderick's wonderful buildings for the city – has been renovated as a shopping centre for specialist outlets and is worth visiting for its soaring architectural splendour alone. Nearby is the Waterloo Antiques Centre, a group of over forty dealers housed in the former Cloth Hall.

Things to Do
TOURIST INFORMATION CENTRE – Wellington Street (turn left out of station and walk 400 yards or so) Tel: Leeds (0532) 478302.
ARMLEY MILLS INDUSTRIAL MUSEUM – see 'Walking'.
THWAITE MILLS – Thwaite Lane, Stourton. Open Tue Sun. Tel: Leeds 496453. Buses 7, 167-9, 410/1 from city centre. Restored watermill on island in the River Aire
MIDDLETON RAILWAY – Moor Road, Hunslet. Sat & Suns April – Sept + Weds in Aug. Tel: Leeds 710324 Buses 59 or 61 from city centre. Industrial locomotives haul short passenger trains over a mile route dating back to 1758.
KIRKSTALL ABBEY & ABBEY HOUSE MUSEUM Kirkstall. 5 minutes from Headingly station. Tel: Leeds 755821. The museum features reconstructed Victorian streets and shops.

Walking
The Museum of Leeds Trail is a 9 mile route, mostly by way of the towpath of the Leeds & Liverpool Canal, from City Square (adjacent to the station) to Rodley in the Aire Valley. Two miles from the city centre it passes ARMLEY MILLS INDUSTRIAL MUSEUM housed in what was once the world's largest woollen mill. The museum (Tel: Leeds 637861) is open daily except for Mondays and there are bus services back to the city centre.

An Historic Plaques Trail starts and ends at the Tourist Information Centre and describes a city centre route around some of Leeds most interesting and historic buildings.

CROSBY GARRETT. *"From the viaduct the village looks beguiling."*

Long Preston

They still hold an annual dance around the maypole at Long Preston, though the days of calico making and cattle trading are long gone. The A65 tends to detract from what would otherwise be a picturesque village with some fine buildings, notably the row of almhouses near the railway.

Refreshments & Accommodation
MAYPOLE INN – village green. Food & accommodation; Les Routiers recommended. Tel: Long Preston (07294) 219.

Shopping
Post office stores.

R
Ribblehead

Not so much a settlement, more the source of the eponymous river in a moorland setting. Informal parking and camping is available beside the B6255 and this activity tends to intrude on the sense of wilderness at the height of the season. But caves and limestone pavements lie within easy reach of the station and you can soon escape from the hot dog stands and unambitious crowds.

Refreshments
THE STATION INN – variety of beers on draught, meals and snacks.

Walking
See 'Walkabout 3'. Also worth considering: the 'Craven Way' across the shoulder of Whernside to Dent (7 miles).

S
Saltaire

Just when you're not expecting it, you come upon Saltaire, one of the most beautiful places in England. This may sound far fetched. After all, this *is* the West Riding, and you *are* on the doorstep of Bradford. But take our word for it, Saltaire comes as an extraordinary surprise. It was laid out as a model community in the mid 19th century by a prosperous and philanthropic mill owner called Sir Titus Salt. The huge 5 storey mill was built in a strategic position between the new railway and the already well established Leeds & Liverpool Canal. On an adjoining greenfield site Sir Titus built a village for his workforce. He also provided a church, an institute, a school, a fire station and a wash house, but no pub! Titus belonged to the Temperance League and had no wish for his workforce to experience the miseries of liquor. The cobbled streets of stone built houses were laid out in a grid pattern and their quiet dignity remains apparent to this day. Saltaire's industrial role has ceased and the village is now a residential community and a growing tourist attraction; though the latter has not, as yet, been permitted to spoil the atmosphere of the place.

Refreshments
VILLAGE TEAROOMS – Victoria Road. Coffee shop, tearooms and restaurant. Charming establishment worth missing the next train for.
BOATHOUSE CAFE – riverside. Snacks, meals and rowing boat hire.
VICTORIA FISHERIES – Victoria Road. Fish & chips.

Shopping
Bakery, mill shop and antiquarian bookshop.

Things to Do
1853 GALLERY – Housed in Salt's mill, exhibits include premier collection of local artist David Hockney. Open daily. Tel: Bradford (0274) 531163.
SHIPLEY GLEN TRAMWAY – 5 minutes walk to northwest of station. Victorian cable tramway offering delightful rides in open carriages up wooded hillside. Open Easter to October weekends, plus Weds in June & July. Tel: Bradford 589010.
ORGAN & HARMONIUM MUSEUM – Victoria Road. Open daily ex Fri & Sat 11am – 4pm.

Walking
Short walks around Saltaire itself. Through Shipley Glen up on to Baildon Moor. Along the towpath of the Leeds & Liverpool Canal towards Shipley or Bingley.

Settle

People tend to use Settle as a launch pad for the railway and so miss much of its intrinsic charm. In fact there are few Yorkshire market towns more captivating than this, and it would be a great pity for you to see no more of it than the view from the train window. Settle is compact, its streets squeezed between the east bank of the Ribble and a huge outcrop of limestone known as the Castleberg. A steep path zig-zags to the top of the rock from which you can see the little town set before you like a model village. From the market square, where the orange and grey Pennine buses stop to set down, and the mountain bikes lie stacked Oxbridge fashion outside Ye Olde Naked Man cafe, you can trace the tight-knit streets and alleys, charting their seemingly haphazard course about the purlieus of the town. You can peer down into back gardens and on to rooftops, simultaneously appreciative of the pattern of play on the bowling green and the movement of fielders on the cricket ground.

Refreshments & Accommodation
YE OLDE NAKED MAN – market place. Formerly an inn dating back to 1663. Now a cafe with adjoining bakery, good for making up picnics.
LIVERPOOL HOUSE – Chapel Square (near post office). A little gem, tucked away from the hurly-burly of the town, its name relates to an abortive plan to build a branch of the Leeds & Liverpool Canal to Settle in the 18th century. The tea room is decorated with displays of domestic memorablia and household linen. Baking is to the highest standard and the cakes are mouthwatering – ask if they have the egg nog flan, Yorkshire courting cake, or fruit slab with Wensleydale cheese. Closed Weds & Thurs. Bed & Breakfast and evening meals by arrangement. Tel: Settle (0729) 822247.

There are numerous other cafes, two fish & chip sho[ps], several pubs, restaurants and a wine bar all situated [in] the town centre just 3 minutes walk from the statio[n]. Some of the pubs offer accommodation, there are lots [of] guest houses, and a large hotel, THE FALCON MAN[OR] (Tel: Settle (0729) 823814) on the southern edge of [the] town – contact the Tourist Information for up to d[ate] details.

Shopping
They've been holding the Tuesday market here since 12[4?] and though most of the stalls have changed, there is s[till] an authentic feel to the proceedings, enlivened by an [ac]cordion player with a sheepdog called Sally. The sta[lls] gather around the old 'shambles', an unusual split le[vel] building with cottages on the top storey and shops [on] two levels below. With barely a supermarket in sig[ht] Settle's shops are run on the old-fashioned precepts [of] courtesy and personal service. There are some truly exc[el]lent bakers and grocers; notably Glynns Gold Medal ba[k]ers on Church Street, a stopping off point for many W[est] Riding folk on their way to and from the Dales and [the] Lakes. As befits a town on the doorstep of the Dales th[ere] are several country pursuits shops, at least two of wh[ich] specialise in climbing and caving equipment. Wednesd[ay] is early closing and there are branches of Barclays, M[id]land, NatWest and TSB banks.

Things to Do
TOURIST INFORMATION CENTRE – Town Hall. T[el:] Settle (0729) 825192 (open mid March to mid Novem[ber] daily).
MUSEUM OF NORTH CRAVEN LIFE – Chapel Stre[et.] Small museum of local history.
See also 'Excursion 3' for the description of a bicycle r[ide] from Settle to Ribblehead via Clapham and Ingleton.

Walking
THE ELGAR WAY – 13 mile circuit of Settle and [the] surrounding limestone countryside incorporating pa[ths] used by Elgar on his visits to Dr Buck, the local G[P.] Descriptive leaflets available locally to this and numero[us] other walks in the vicinity.

Bus Connections
Pennine Motors services link Settle with Giggleswick (e[as]ily walkable anyway), Clapham and Ingleton. Tel: Sk[ip]ton (0756) 749215.

Silsden

This unexpectedly appealing former mill town reta[ins] some modern vestiges of the textile industry. A tribut[ary] of the Aire keeps close attendance with the High Str[eet,] lending considerable charm to what is usually a bustl[ing] thoroughfare fronted by solidly stone built shops a[nd] banks and miscellaneous commercial premises. The Le[eds] & Liverpool Canal – which presumably played its p[art] in the growth of local industry – passes through the to[wn] and holidaymakers can set off on luxury narrowbo[ats] from here to explore the canal on its way across [the]

LANGWATHBY MOOR. *"the River Eamont makes an entrance, its confluence with the Eden occuring amidst broad meadows . . ."*

Pennines into Lancashire. Note that the town centre is about 15 minutes walk from Steeton & Silsden station, though there are frequent buses.

Refreshments
Plenty of pubs and seemingly more than its fair share of take-aways, from the traditional Yorkshire fish & chips to Italian pizzas.

Shopping
Hardly a supermarket or chain store in sight, but lots of refreshingly individual corner shops like Hills the baker and Holgates the grocer. Barclays and Nat West banks and post office.

Things to Do
Day boat hire on the Leeds & Liverpool Canal from Silsden Boats. Further details on Steeton (0535) 53675.

Walking
Pleasant walks along the towpath of the canal to Riddlesden (NT hall to visit) and Bingley.

Shipley
The best things about Shipley are the Sooty centre and the waterbus and, unfortunately, other than the remarkable triangular station, there is little else for the casual visitor to enthuse over. The town itself is centred on the 'very Sixties' Arndale shopping centre and market, so architecturally abhorrent that it is almost charming. Refreshments are more or less restricted to cheap cafes and Chinese take-aways, though one pub of possible interest to thirsty railway fans is "The Sun Hotel", which has a rooftop patio offering grandstand views over the Skipton platform.

Things to Do
THE WORLD & SOOTY – Leeds Road, 5 minutes from station. Open daily. Tel: (0274) 531122. Memorablilia dating back to the first Sooty show in 1952 when Harry Corbett's was the hand inside the cheeky glove puppet.

Nowadays his son, Matthew, is more or less in control of Sooty, Sweep, Sue and the rest. Children will love it, adults be transported back to their own childhood.
METRO WATERBUS – Sunday and Bank Holiday Monday service by 'barge' along the Leeds & Liverpool Canal between Shipley, Saltaire and Bingley. Tel: (0274) 595914 for timings, fares etc. See also 'Excursion 1'.

Skipton
Old 'Sheep Town' still holds sway over the Aire Gap as it has done since the 7th century. The development of communications have helped it to thrive: turnpike, canal, railway and modern road have each brought periods of prosperity down the ages. The centre of town is about 5 minutes walk from the station. Quite the best way in is along the towpath of the Leeds & Liverpool Canal, a well-surfaced, traffic-free approach past former textile mills seeing new industrial use or conversion to flats. If the canal casts its spell on you there are boats to be hired or public trips to be made, whilst if you have a deeper interest in waterways you could do worse than explore the little Springs Branch which led to a quarry under the ramparts of the castle.

Refreshments & Accommodation
BLACK HORSE HOTEL – High Street. Old coaching inn serving bar and restaurant food. Younger's and Theakston beer and accommodation. Tel: Skipton (0756) 792145.
WATERSIDE COTTAGE TEAROOMS – Coach Street. Coffees, lunches and teas.
BIZZIE LIZZIES – Belmont Bridge. Fish & chip restaurant & take-away.
TOM JONES – Albert Street. Carvery restaurant housed in former wool warehouse.
THE WINE BARN – Victoria Street. open daily, 11am – 11pm for anything from a glass of wine to a full meal.

Shopping
Skipton is an excellent shopping centre and has attracted the likes of Rackhams, Laura Ashley and the Edinburgh

Woollen Mill to open branches here. Market stalls line the wide High Street every day of the week with the exception of Tuesday and Sunday. Many alleyways issue from the High Street and lead to interesting courtyards, most notably Craven Court, an alley which opens out into an airy rectangle covered by a graceful canopy of cast iron and glass. As well as the chain stores there are lots of individual shops of charm such as Stanforth's 'celebrated pork pie establishment' on Mill Bridge. More prosaically, but conveniently practical, is a large Morrison supermarket handily located beside the railway station. Most of the main banks are represented, whilst some shops close on Wednesday afternoons.

Things To Do
SKIPTON CASTLE – top of High Street. The town's crowning glory, a superb 11th century fortification, birthplace of Lady Anne Clifford. Open daily from 10am (2pm Sundays). Tel: Skipton (0756) 792442
CRAVEN MUSEUM – Town Hall. Local history.
PENNINE CRUISERS – Coach Street. Tel: Skipton (0756) 795478. Motorised canal boats for hire by the day along a 17 mile lock-free section of the Leeds & Liverpool Canal.
PENNINE BOAT TRIPS – Coach Street. Tel: Skipton (0756) 790829. Public trips aboard the 'wide boat' Cobbydale along the canal, usually daily during the summer.
EMBSAY STEAM RAILWAY – 2 miles east of Skipton; bus connections – see below. Tel: Skipton (0756) 794727. Trains run on Sundays throughout the year, on Sats & Tues in July, and daily (ex Mon & Fri) in August. The return trip takes 40 minutes. Embsay station includes a well stocked railway bookshop and cafe and there's a picnic area at Holywell Halt.

Bus Connections
Keighley & District buses run to the picturesque village of Grassington in Wharfedale. Tel: Skipton (0756) 795331 for timings.
Pennine Motors serve Malham (for the Cove, Tarn & Gordale Scar) and Embsay (for Embsay Steam Railway). Tel: Skipton (0756) 749215 for timings.

LOW HOUSE CROSSING. *"encountering in the process a rare level crossing, and passing the 300 mile marker from St Pancras."*

INFORMATION

Scheduled Services

Ordinary service trains operate throughout the year between Leeds, Settle and Carlisle. On Mondays to Saturdays an average of six trains are run in each direction, whilst an additional train runs at the height of the summer season, and there is also an early morning service to Leeds from Ribblehead and an evening service from Leeds to Horton. On Sundays there are three trains in each direction between Leeds and Carlisle. All of these trains call at all stations between Settle and Carlisle and one or two of them call additionally at Gargrave, Hellifield and Long Preston; though most trains calling at these three stations run between Leeds and Morecambe. Between Leeds and Skipton trains run half-hourly Monday to Saturday and hourly on Sunday. There is also an hourly Mon-Sat service from Bradford to Skipton which runs bi-hourly on Sundays.

It is not possible to list departure times of the above-mentioned services here, as these may alter during the currency of this guidebook. The average journey time between Leeds and Carlisle is just over two and a half hours; between Settle and Carlisle it is around an hour and three-quarters. Leeds, Settle & Carlisle line timetables are widely available throughout the area that the line runs through and from most British Rail travel centres. Telephone Leeds (0532) 448133 or Carlisle (0228) 44711 for further details and timetable enquiries. Local enquiries can be made during working hours to the stations at Settle (0729 – 823536) and Appleby (07683 – 51434).

Tickets

The simplest form of ticket available for use on the Leeds, Settle & Carlisle line is the 'cheap day return'. This can be purchased for travel out and back on the same day from any of the stations along the line. For unrestricted travel between Settle and Carlisle and any of the intermediate stations, a 'Day Ranger' ticket is available. 'Round Robin' tickets are available from London Euston, the Midlands and the North for day tours of the Lancaster – Carlisle – Skipton circuit on Mondays – Thursdays and Saturdays. Various 'Rover' tickets are available on a 4 days out of 8 basis which cover travel over the Settle & Carlisle. Seats can be reserved on most services, ask at your local BR office for further details.

Between Settle and Carlisle the only station with a ticket office is Appleby. Passengers boarding at all the other stations en route must purchase their tickets on the train. Similarly, the stations southwards from Settle at Long Preston, Hellifield and Gargrave, Cononley, Steeton & Silsden, Crossflatts and Saltaire are unstaffed and tickets must be bought on the train. Scheduled trains operating between Leeds, Settle and Carlisle offer Standard Class accommodation only. Seats can be reserved on most services for up to four people travelling together. Telephone Leeds or Carlisle stations for details.

Charter Trains

Three organisations operate regular charter excursions over the Settle & Carlisle line.

FLYING SCOTSMAN SERVICES (Tel: Carnforth (0524) 734220) run "The Cumbrian Mountain Express" from London Euston to Appleby via Blackburn, from which point it is steam hauled. A second steam locomotive hauls the train back from Appleby to Blackburn. Boarding points for this service, which runs on Saturdays approximately twenty times a year, are currently Euston, Watford, Milton Keynes, Nuneaton, Crewe, Wigan and Blackburn.

British Rail's own INTERCITY Charter Unit operate several diesel-hauled 'Day Out' (Tel:071-388 0519) or 'Land Cruise' (Tel: Lichfield (0543) 254076) itineraries incorporating travel over the Settle & Carlisle line. Leaflets listing routes and dates of these excursions are widely available at British Rail Travel Centres.

HERTFORDSHIRE RAIL TOURS (Tel: Welwyn (043 871) 5050) operate 'Luxury Days Out' using 125 High Speed Trains over the Settle & Carlisle railway from various centres in the South-east and the Midlands.

Guided Walks

A programme of guided walks led by local experts operates on most Saturdays throughout the year. The walk leader meets ramblers at a pre-designated station and leads them (for a modest charge of around £1 adults and 50p children) on a walk of between 10 and 15 miles through some of the most appealing countryside in the Yorkshire Dales. Many of the routes are circular and you catch the train back from the same station you alighted at. Others are of a linear nature and you travel back from another station along the line. Details and dates of the walks usually appear in the British Rail timetable leaflet, or you can telephone Clapham (04685) 419 for further details. Other organisations also arrange guided walks and you should look out for local information regarding these.

Bicycles

Since 'Sprinter' diesel units took over most services on the Settle & Carlisle in 1990 facilities for the carriage of bicycles are somewhat restricted. Strictly speaking space for the carriage of a bicycle should be reserved in advance and a fee of £3 (1991 price) is payable. You can make a reservation at any staffed BR station in the country.

Without a reservation you may possibly be able to make informal arrangements with the guard of a Settle-Carlisle train to carry your bike, but such an undertaking would be at his discretion, depending on whether or not there is room on the train.

On METRO trains between Leeds and Giggleswick, bicycles can be carried free of charge where space is available, except for some peak hour services.

Useful Contacts

Friends of the Settle & Carlisle Line

"The Friends" were formed in 1981 to campaign against the threatened closure of the Settle & Carlisle railway. When the line was reprieved in 1989 the group changed their attention to promoting the railway to ensure long-term success. FOSCL members look after the unstaffed stations between Settle and Carlisle and advertise services throughout the area. Membership of FOSCL cludes a quarterly newsletter. Further details from current secretary: Ian Rodham, Flat 2, 37B Bath Stre Abingdon OX14 7RH.

Settle & Carlisle Trust

A charity formed in 1991 to assist financially with restoration of historic structures along the line, and promote public knowledge and understanding of heritage significance of the line. Corporate and individ donations are welcomed. Further details from: S&C Ra way Trust, The Railway Station, Broughton Road, Sk ton, N. Yorks BD23 1RT. Tel: Skipton (0756) 79608

Transport Users Consultative Committee

Should you have any complaints or comments regardi services on the Leeds, Settle & Carlisle line which Brit Rail are unable to deal adequately or appropriately wi then you can take the matter up with the local TUC Responsibility for the line is split between the North E England TUCC of Hilary House, St Saviour's Place, Yo YO1 2PL, and the North Western England TUCC Room 112, Boulton House, 17-21 Chorlton Street, Ma chester M1 3HY.

Steam Operations

A recorded information service for steam enthusiasts, gi ing details of steam excursion dates and timings (use for photographers) is available on 0898 88 1968.

Weather

The locals will tell you take Met Office predictions w a pinch of salt up in the Dales, but you might be reassur (or misled) by listening to the recorded forecast on following number 0839 500 417.

Further Reading

Numerous railway enthusiast orientated books, coveri many aspects of the Settle & Carlisle line have been pu lished over the years, and those still in print are wide available from specialist outlets regularly advertised various enthusiast magazines. Likewise, there is a host literature covering the topography of the West Ridi Yorkshire Dales and Eden Valley, and most towns these districts sport booksellers and Tourist Informati Centres which stock a good selection of these. Two ti published locally (Leading Edge Press of Burterse Hawes) of interest to users of the line are: "Settle Carlisle Country" by Colin Speakman and John Morris which describes the 150 mile 'Settle – Carlisle Way notional route of public footpaths linking Leeds with C lisle; and "The Line that Refused to Die" by Stan Abb and Alan Whitehouse, the story of the campaign to sa the line from closure in the 1980s: Leading Edge a publish the "Leeds, Settle & Carlisle Express", a f sheet widely available along the line listing current eve and full of useful advertisements.